AKRON ART MUSEUM
JANUARY 23 – MAY 9, 2010

KEMPER MUSEUM OF CONTEMPORARY ART
JANUARY 28 – MAY 8, 2011

PATTERN

ID

MARK BRADFORD

IONA ROZEAL BROWN

NICK CAVE

WILLIE COLE

LALLA ESSAYDI

SAMUEL FOSSO

JAMES GOBEL

BRIAN JUNGEN

BHARTI KHER

TAKASHI MURAKAMI

GRACE NDIRITU

YINKA SHONIBARE, MBE

MICKALENE THOMAS

AYA UEKAWA

KEHINDE WILEY

ELLEN RUDOLPH
WITH AN ESSAY BY
CECILIA GUNZBURGER ANDERSON

PATTERN ID

THIS EXHIBITION IS MADE POSSIBLE WITH GENEROUS SUPPORT FROM

AKRON COMMUNITY FOUNDATION
NATIONAL ENDOWMENT FOR THE ARTS
HERB AND DIANNE NEWMAN
JOHN S. AND JAMES L. KNIGHT FOUNDATION
TOBY D. LEWIS PHILANTHROPIC FUND

THE KEMPER MUSEUM IS GRATEFUL FOR PATTERN ID CATALOGUE
SUPPORT FROM LYNN ADKINS AND LINDA LIGHTON

FOREWORD

This visually enthralling exhibition organized by Curator of Exhibitions Ellen Rudolph stands in brilliant contrast to much art of recent generations that has addressed similar concerns. Cultural, gender and ethnic identity issues emerged in conceptual, feminist and performance art during the 1970s and were given an even stronger focus in the 1990s, but those works rarely evinced the visual splendor and reworking of historical precedents so obvious in *Pattern ID*. Aesthetically, the artists gathered together in *Pattern ID* perhaps share certain interests with the short-lived Pattern and Decoration movement of the late 1970s, an American reaction against conceptual art that was strongly influenced by feminism.

The new work represented in this exhibition, however, spans global practice, multiple ethnic groups and divergent historical perspectives. It brings those earlier concerns into a complex new century and to the forefront of current artistic practice. The widespread attention to the artists in this exhibition from print media, museums and commercial galleries worldwide makes it clear that these artists are addressing seminal issues in contemporary art and culture. Their chosen vehicles for talking about cultural identity— pattern and dress—speak to the continuing power of some of the most common visual phenomena in all cultures.

The subject of contemporary artists' use of textiles and patterns has been looked at in such contexts as African art and in terms of feminism but has not yet been surveyed on a broader scale. The cross-pollination of aesthetic traditions in *Pattern ID* reaches across time, culture and geography to meld fine art and popular culture in a very satisfying way.

The past decade has been thrilling for the contemporary art world. After decades of domination by West European and U.S. artists and institutions, modern artistic practice has become fully global. Countries formerly isolated in artistic practice have produced some of the best artists working today. There has been an explosion of fairs and biennials around the world, from Cuenca and Cairo to Seoul and Shanghai, offering competition to the venerable biennials in Venice and São Paulo. Even those traditional venues have changed, as artists from the southern hemisphere, Asia and the Near East claim prominent roles.

Artists have probably been itinerants for millennia, at least from the time of Alexander. But today artists maintain hectic international schedules that rival those of secretaries of state and top corporate executives. As artists travel—

working, immigrating, vacationing, teaching—they incorporate new experiences into their native artistic traditions, in turn fertilizing new cultures.

It is impossible for the broader public to ignore the range of questions around cultural identity that artists are raising, especially when they reveal the nuances of how people today embrace, accumulate and shed various identities. They open our eyes by illustrating just how fluid "identity" is and how it may sometimes be a constructed rather than natural phenomenon.

I trust readers will enjoy the two essays in this publication. Ellen Rudolph discusses the ways in which artists borrow from art historical works and motifs, world history and styles of dress in popular culture, all with the goal of activating dialogue about their cultural identity. In the second essay, textile and fashion historian Cecilia Gunzburger Anderson describes the cultural origins of many of the textiles that appear in *Pattern ID*.

The presentation of this exhibition in Akron is especially appropriate, as this city has embraced a global perspective since the birth of the tire industry more than a century ago. Today, it is a world leader in polymer research and production, welcoming scholars and businesses from around the globe. Dr. Barbara Tannenbaum and I have sought to collect works for the museum's collection by contemporary artists of varied ethnicity, education, gender, race, sexual orientation and geographic origin. In recent years, we have had a special interest in artists from Japan and sub-Saharan Africa, amplifying our historical focus on American artists. This exhibition has allowed us the gratifying opportunity to add to our collections a major painting by Mickalene Thomas, a monumental photograph by Yinka Shonibare and additional work by Samuel Fosso, who received the museum's 2006 Knight Purchase Award for Photographic Media.

All of us at the Akron Art Museum are enormously grateful to the artists and the many lenders to this exhibition. Without the artists' acumen and our lenders' impressive generosity, there would be no exhibition. To our selfless funders, I offer my deepest appreciation, for your philanthropy has created the opportunity for immensely talented individuals to display their ideas in a vital public forum. I especially thank Akron Community Foundation, Dianne and Herbert Newman, Dr. Gerald Austen and the Knight Foundation and Toby Devan Lewis, all longtime friends and supporters of the museum.

Thanks to the keen interest of Curator Barbara O'Brien and the support of Director and CEO Rachael Blackburn Cozad, I am thrilled that *Pattern ID* will travel to the distinguished Kemper Museum of Contemporary Art in Kansas City, Missouri. An institution that aims to foster greater understanding of the human experience through exchange and dialogue, the Kemper is perfectly suited to extend the experience of this extraordinary exhibition to its diverse community.

Art museums are devoted to the arrangement of objects. The favorite word of those who work in museums is "juxtaposition." We can't give a speech or write an essay without using the word, because museums are fundamentally about that concept: comparing and contrasting aspects of one work with another. This exhibition not only juxtaposes artists and works from different cultures, but each individual object exemplifies within itself that central museological concept of providing a new revelation when different points of view meet.

Mitchell Kahan, Ph.D.
Director & CEO
Akron Art Museum

The Kemper Museum of Contemporary Art is pleased and proud to host *Pattern ID*. This mesmerizing dialogue concerning decoration, codification, and identity is a project fitting to our mission to represent national and international aesthetic and cultural diversity. Kansas City, home of the Kemper Museum, was during its formative years a trading post and gateway to the West; today it is a geographic junction for national and international trade by rail, air, and interstate highway. We are grateful to the Akron Art Museum, the artists represented herein, and the curatorial expertise behind *Pattern ID*, for so vibrantly reminding us that we are all forever at our own crossroads.

Rachael Blackburn Cozad
Director and CEO
Kemper Museum of Contemporary Art

A C K N O W L E D G M E N T S

8

I offer my gratitude to all the artists for creating fresh, continuously inspiring work and for their enthusiastic participation in *Pattern ID*. In addition, I extend a warm thank you to all the donors and lenders to the exhibition without whose generosity this project would not have been possible.

My thanks to Jack Shainman, Claude Simard and Sabrina Vanderputt at Jack Shainman Gallery for their time, patience and support of the exhibition. I am deeply appreciative of Sarah Aibel, the Sender Collection; Jordan Buscher, Mickalene Thomas Studio; Julie Castellano, Edwynn Houk Gallery; Lindsay Charlwood, Roberts & Tilton; Jane Cohan, James Cohan Gallery; Susie Kravets and Marc Wehby, Kravets/Wehby; Amy Levin, Alexander and Bonin; Carrie Mackin, Kehinde Wiley Studio; Meg Malloy, Sikkema Jenkins & Co.; Charlotte Marra and Rhona Hoffman, Rhona Hoffman Gallery; Lauren Miller, Sandroni Rey; Loring Randolph, Casey Kaplan; Jessica Sain, Goff + Rosenthal; Adrian Turner, Marianne Boesky Gallery; and Nicola Vassell, Deitch Projects for their assistance in locating works for the exhibition.

The entire staff of the Akron Art Museum provided support and assistance, but I am particularly grateful to Mitchell Kahan and Barbara Tannenbaum for championing *Pattern ID* and for their expert guidance. I warmly thank Arnie Tunstall, Missy Higgins-Linder, Alison Caplan, Allison Tillinger Schmid, Joe Walton, Craig Arnold, and Gina Thomas McGee for their generous input, excitement and encouragement. Thanks also to Lynne Van Nostran for her grant writing and to curatorial interns Annaliese Soden and Laura Rother for their crucial contributions in researching and organizing the exhibition catalogue.

Textile and fashion historian Cecilia Gunzburger Anderson brought valuable expertise and fascinating insights to the catalogue in her essay *We Are What We Wear*. Thanks to Christopher Hoot for matching the energy of the artwork with a dynamic and innovative book design.

I am grateful to Toby Devan Lewis and Ellen Landau, whose passion, knowledge, energy and enthusiasm have inspired me deeply.

Ellen Rudolph
Curator of Exhibitions

AKRON ART MUSEUM
ALEXANDER AND BONIN
DANNY FIRST
GLENN FUHRMAN
STEPHEN HEIGHTON
EDWYNN HOUK GALLERY
CASEY KAPLAN
KRAVETS/WEHBY
CHRISTOPHER MELTON
GRACE NDIRITU
RICHARD PRICE
THE PROGRESSIVE CORPORATION
DAVID A. SACHS AND KAREN RICHARDS SACHS
ANN AND MEL SCHAFFER FAMILY COLLECTION
SENDER COLLECTION
SHAHEEN MODERN AND CONTEMPORARY ART
JACK SHAINMAN AND CLAUDE SIMARD
JACK SHAINMAN GALLERY

LENDERS TO THE EXHIBITION

SIKKEMA JENKINS & CO.
RANBIR SINGH
THE SPEED ART MUSEUM
MICKALENE THOMAS
ALISON AND LAWRENCE WOLFSON

THE CULTURAL CURRENCY OF PATTERN AND DRESS

Ellen Rudolph

Hans Holbein the Younger, *The Ambassadors*, 1533. Oil on oak, 81 1/2 x 82 1/2 in. National Gallery, London.

Henri Matisse, *Reclining Odalisque in Gray Culottes*, 1927. Oil on canvas, 25 5/8 x 32 in. The Metropolitan Museum of Art, New York, the Walter H. and Leonore Annenberg Collection, Gift of Walter H. and Leonore Annenberg, 1997, Bequest of Walter H. Annenberg, 2002 (1997.4).

Miriam Schapiro, *Wonderland,* 1983. Acrylic, fabric, plastic beads on canvas, 90 x 144 1/2 in. Smithsonian American Art Museum, Washington, D.C., gift of an anonymous donor (1996.88).

Certain patterns are unmistakable: the neatly arranged vines of damask wallpaper, or the interlocking initials of the Louis Vuitton monogram. But explode the classically sober brown and tan Louis Vuitton pattern into bright colors, or pair damask wallpaper patterns with oversized hip-hop clothing and the cultural meanings of these patterns are transformed. Their wearers bear the markings of newly formed identities. Over the past two decades, artists have increasingly turned to pattern and dress as a visual language with which to communicate who they are.

Artists have in fact been signaling time, place and identity through pattern and dress for centuries. Wealth, power, status, nationality and ethnicity, along with access and relationships to other cultures, can all be implied by an artist's use of textiles and clothing. In Hans Holbein's *The Ambassadors,* the Anatolian carpet draped over the table and the green silk damask backdrop evidence travel and wealth at a time of developing world colonialism.[1]

Among art history's noted purveyors of textile patterns, Henri Matisse painted still lives and odalisques that convey his passion for decorative pattern and motifs. In the early twentieth century, Matisse visited Algeria and Morocco—then French colonies—where he was inspired by the brilliant light, exotic setting and Moorish architecture. He incorporated the patterns and styles of dress he saw there into paintings that re-created his fantasy of the harem.[2]

Fast forwarding to the 1970s and early 1980s, artists of the Pattern and Decoration movement brought textiles and patterns derived from craft, design and non-Western art forms into the realm of fine art. These artists' interest in pattern and decoration spawned from such varied influences as women's handiwork and Islamic design. Like Matisse, they were largely borrowing these motifs as outsiders, but they aimed to broaden the cultural vocabulary of contemporary art.

The artists in *Pattern ID* use pattern and dress to take up the twenty-first-century challenge of locating one's place in society against the backdrop of globalization. *Pattern ID* brings together fifteen artists who use their art to help negotiate cultural identity. While many of them mine their transcultural experiences, be they national, ethnic, racial, socioeconomic, political or religious, several also examine the influence of society on gender roles and their own sexuality.

Many transplants feel they no longer fit in within their culture of origin, nor are they totally at home in their new environment. Lalla Essaydi, for example, a Moroccan artist who lived in Saudi Arabia for several years and now lives in the United States, recounts, "When I'm in Saudi Arabia, they call me the Moroccan. In Morocco, they call me the Saudi. In the West, I am someone from a different culture."[3]

The artists in *Pattern ID* represent themselves in uniquely layered ways. Rather than trade one identity for another, they reveal ways in which identity can be cumulative, a result of moving in and out of various cultural milieux. These artists respond to the challenge of being in between, as cultural theorist Homi Bhabha has described, by transcending cultural categories "to show how the system of world knowledges is deeply intersected."[4] Among the ways artists have achieved this transcendence is through their use of pattern and dress, two primary means of communicating identity.[5] They mix patterns and styles from art, world history and popular culture, while combining artistic genres to create pastiches of time, place and identity.

Although the work in *Pattern ID* defies simple categorization, some of the major themes through which the artists explore the complexities of their cultural identities include art historical appropriation, gender identity, cultural intersections, mapping cultural heritage and utopias. It must be noted, though, that most of the works can be considered in the context of several of these topics, not to mention other thematic dialogues that the gathering of these artists will surely spark.

Appropriating Art History

Because the canon of art history assumes a Western perspective, picturing cultural identity through its lens provides a convenient point of contrast or comparison. Several of the artists in *Pattern ID* challenge the accuracy and completeness of the canon as a historical and cultural record by re-presenting iconic works in ways that point to nuances of race, gender and ethnicity that art history has omitted. Notably, many of the artists borrow from within and outside their own cultural traditions at the same time, aware of how their cultures have been depicted from both vantage points.

Kehinde Wiley's paintings are based primarily on Old Master portraits from the sixteenth through nineteenth centuries. For each of his portraits, he invites his sitters,

young black men he meets on the streets of major urban centers, to strike a pose from an art historical painting. The choices Wiley offers his sitters are regal portraits of noblemen, royalty, religious figures and heroes who typically hail from the era of European imperialism. Wiley photographs his subjects in their street clothes or hip-hop gear he provides and then paints them amid decorative, richly patterned backgrounds. Often ornately framed, his portraits mix time, culture and race to recast historical figures as young black men.

Although Wiley presents his sitters in positions of importance, the patterned backgrounds simultaneously endow and threaten the men's power and masculinity. *Alexander the Great*, a new version of history's most infamous war hero, communicates a mix of toughness, defiance, aggression, authority and power. But Wiley creates a provocative tension between the figure's bold attitude and the background by suggestively curling a stray vine from the swirling botanical pattern that frames him over his body and around his sword. Likewise, the brilliant orange background and pink roses of the rococo-esque pattern in *The Blessing Christ* compete with the figure, while a bouquet of roses conceals his groin. Wiley deliberately plays on the identity transfer that takes place through the models' translation of their historical precedents' poses. He states, "[The models] are assuming the poses of colonial masters, the former bosses of the Old World."[6] In this way, he embeds in his portraits a complicated relationship between historical power and the contemporary street culture that he portrays.

12

Kehinde Wiley, *Alexander the Great*, 2007 (detail of p. 34).

Charles Boit, *Augustus II the Strong* (detail), 1711. Enamel on copper. Gruenes Gewoelbe, Staatliche Kunstsammlungen, Dresden, Germany.

Kehinde Wiley, *The Blessing Christ*, 2007 (detail of p. 66).

The hip-hop culture represented in Wiley's paintings takes on an entirely different tone in iona rozeal brown's work. In her a3 [afro-asiatic allegories] blackface series, brown uses the flattened, linear style and compositional format of traditional ukiyo-e (literally, "pictures of the floating world") woodblock prints to portray Japanese teens' co-option of hip-hop culture. brown was inspired to visit Japan and better understand the *ganguro* (literally, "black face girls") after reading journalist Joe Wood's 1997 article "The Yellow Negro."[7] Wood discussed the ramifications of the fashion trend popular in the 1990s in which young Japanese women darkened their skin and bleached and permed their hair to mimic the style of African-American hip-hop stars.

brown exposes parallels between contemporary ganguro and the high fashions, codes of behavior and excesses of the floating world (the historical red light district). She connects Japanese teens' idealized view of hip-hop culture as a new, independent mode of expression to the world pictured in ukiyo-e prints, a world removed from the restrictions of everyday life.[8] In *a3 blackface #67*, brown offers a fresh version of Kitagawa Utamaro's eighteenth-century print *The Hairdresser* from the series "Twelve Female Professions." Just as coiffures and kimono patterns were highly codified in the floating world, the afro picks on the attendant's kimono indicate his role as the hairstylist, while the client's fur-trimmed pink leopard-print hoodie suggests her coquettish availability.

brown's play on race can be read in many ways. Her rendering of blackface reverses the geisha, whose faces were painted white. Historically, white powder on Japanese women's faces symbolized womanhood and beauty. Blackface in American culture refers to the theatrical makeup worn in the nineteenth and early twentieth centuries by white actors who portrayed black characters in a stereotypically racist manner. Presumably contemporary Japanese teens who darkened their faces were unaware of the racist implications in the United States, ironically using the practice as a form of rebellion against their culture's conservative traditions. In showing us how the meanings of cultural signs change when translated from West to East, brown sheds new light on racism, rebellion, mimicry and coolness.

Gender Identity Challenges Art History

Several artists in *Pattern ID* use art history to rework traditional gender dynamics between artist and sitter and between sitter and viewer. Kehinde Wiley's portraits express tension between masculine and feminine roles. Although his models pose authoritatively in their regal patterned backgrounds, a palpable vulnerability seeps into their expressions. Perhaps this is because Wiley's models assume a role traditionally relegated to female subjects—they are the object of the male gaze; the artist

Thomas addresses exoticized stereotypes of black femininity while also exploring how her women fit into art history, which has traditionally relegated black women to subservient, peripheral roles. She looks at black female sexuality from her perspective as an African-American woman whose notions of beauty and femininity were formed while she was growing up in New Jersey in the 1970s and 1980s. Influenced by her stylish mother (a former fashion model), imagery in *Jet* and *Ebony* magazines, 1970s funk and soul music and

Kehinde Wiley, *The Dead Christ on the Tomb*, 2007 (detail of p. 58).

Henri Matisse, *The Pink Studio (Studio of the Painter)*, 1911. Oil on canvas, 70 1/2 x 87 in. Pushkin Museum of Fine Arts, Moscow.

Mickalene Thomas, *A Moments Pleasure #2*, 2008 (see also p. 39).

poses them and then attentively recreates their bodies in paint.[9] Wiley eroticizes their display of male power by accentuating their muscles and smooth skin. In doing so he not only confronts the absence of black male bodies in art history by asserting their beauty, but he also offsets the often-threatening portrayal of the black male body in contemporary American society.[10] On depicting his subjects as objects of desire, Wiley comments: "There is something very sexualized about it. Desire has a lot to do with that."[11] Taking on art history as well as contemporary racial stereotypes, Wiley's promotion of his models' sex appeal creates a tantalizing play on beauty and power.

The art historical genre of the odalisque is used by both Mickalene Thomas and Lalla Essaydi to reconfigure female identity in their respective cultures. The term "odalisque" refers to a female slave or concubine in a harem. In art historical language, odalisque has come to refer to the pose of a reclining woman whose nudity, clothing or surroundings make her exotic.

trips to the Metropolitan Museum of Art, Thomas unites personal experience, popular culture and art history in her rhinestone-encrusted paintings.

Like the "oriental" alcoves Matisse arranged in his Nice apartment, in her studio Thomas assembles domestic interior sets chock full of 1960s and 1970s patterns. She then photographs her models, who are decked out in flamboyant patterned clothing, in these rich environments, basing her paintings on collages of these photographs. Decorative and on display like Matisse's odalisques, Thomas's women, by contrast, appear to have command of their surroundings and the viewer. In *A Moment's Pleasure #2*, the women are languid, casual in their poses. Staring out at the viewer and gazing off in another direction, the two women's indifferent attitudes contrast with the typically self-conscious French odalisque who exists to please her viewer.

In the monumental *Girlfriends and Lovers*, time and place slip back and forth depending on where you look, and diverse cultural and art historical references abound. The repertoire of patterns and textures ranges from AfroEgyptian-style textiles to black-and-white tile reminiscent of fifteenth-century Dutch Old Master painting and wood parquet floors typical of seventeenth-century European interiors. Seated behind a carpet-draped table, Thomas's women supplant the men in Rembrandt van Rijn's *Syndics of the Clothmakers' Guild*. If not pre-eminent cloth manufacturers, the women nonetheless deliver style and attitude. Thomas's models in *Girlfriends and Lovers* are less physically available to the viewer than her odalisques, yet they are equally provocative and alluring in their ultra-feminine dress and postures ranging from demure to confident. Taken together, the shallow curtained stage setting, bold sexuality of the women and geometric forms in the floor evoke Pablo Picasso's groundbreakingly confrontational masterwork, *Les Demoiselles d'Avignon*.

Thomas's evocation of Matisse and Picasso harks back to the colonial era of the early twentieth century, when black female sexuality was portrayed as exotic and enticing yet something to be feared.[12] A black woman, Thomas seizes control of this image, seeking out models who emanate an independent and self-assured sexuality. The poise of her models contrasts with the unease that Kehinde Wiley's decorative backgrounds engender.

Like Thomas, Moroccan native Lalla Essaydi turns the Western orientalist lens onto itself to look at the historically exoticized portrayal of Muslim women. Through her photographs, Essaydi seeks to broaden the narrow Western image of Muslim women as repressed and silent while revisiting her own upbringing in an Islamic country. She brings female Arab friends to her former home in Morocco (now unoccupied), where she drapes them with robes, arranges them in the empty rooms and then photographs them, often recreating compositions of nineteenth-century orientalist paintings. Essaydi covers every surface of the setting, including the women's skin, with calligraphic writings that bespeak her own life experiences. Painstakingly applied in henna, these writings represent both male and female traditions in Islamic culture, for calligraphy is strictly a male practice, while henna designs are used and applied exclusively by women. While Essaydi confines her models to their "proper" place inside the home, she allows them the unusual freedom to speak publicly through their poses and adornment.

Les Femmes du Maroc: Grande Odalisque has the same title and composition as the 1814 painting by Jean-Auguste-Dominique Ingres. The seductive reclining pose of Essaydi's model, however, undermines the deeply ingrained suppression of female sexuality within Islamic culture, while at the same time evoking Western fascination with the odalisque, the veil and the harem. These opposing views of Arab female identity spring from Essaydi's experiences living in both the East and the West. She claims that it is only from her current

state of independence and mobility that she can consider the landscape of her childhood with detachment and understanding. "My work gives me a sense of belonging that I couldn't find in a physical place."[13]

While Essaydi's women quietly express their sexuality via the written word, James Gobel's men make visible the relatively unseen "bear" subculture of the gay community through pattern and material. Gobel's genre scenes of hairy, bearded, large-bellied men dressed in working-class clothing play on the notion that homosexuality conflicts with masculinity by countering the pervasive stereotype of the fit, hairless, highly styled gay man.

Gobel's images reinforce the difficulty of distinguishing bears' masculinity from that of straight men. The plaid shirts and blue jeans in *The Fitting No. 1* and *The Fitting No. 2* suggest the everyday clothing of blue-collar workers, yet these men are fashion designers. They are distinctly low key in attitude and appearance, not the usual image of men in the glamorous, frenetic setting of the gay-dominated fashion world. Gobel also plays on the interaction between his figures' sexuality and the materials he uses: felt and yarn link his paintings to feminine homemade handicrafts. As in Essaydi's work, the style, patterns and materials hold different meanings for different viewers depending on gender, ethnicity and cultural affiliation.

In *I'll Be Your Friend, I'll Be Your Love, I'll Be Everything You Need*, Gobel effects a push and pull between ideals of gay and straight masculinity.[14] Here the heavy-set performer sports the usual bear plaid shirt over an Iron Maiden t-shirt, but the campy leopard-print and rhinestone smoking jacket, along with the phallic pink-tipped microphone, conjure a Liberace-esque lounge singer. His moustache is another bear sign, but its curlicue decorativeness and his pretty, long-lashed eyes offer an effeminate contradiction. Gobel illustrates the pitfalls of attempting to categorize people by literally layering contrasting stereotyped identities.

Cultural Mash-ups

Many of the artists in *Pattern ID* use their work to navigate their own experiences living at the juncture of two cultures. These artists address the issue of how one incorporates the aesthetics, politics, social mores and/or religion of two different cultures into their being.

Takashi Murakami leads a generation of Japanese artists whose work illustrates a search for identity within the pervasive popular-culture forces of anime (computer-

Lalla Essaydi, *Les Femmes du Maroc: Grande Odalisque*, 2008 (detail of p. 36).

Jean-Auguste-Dominique Ingres, *The Great Odalisque*, 1814. Oil on canvas, 36 x 64 in. Musée du Louvre, Paris.

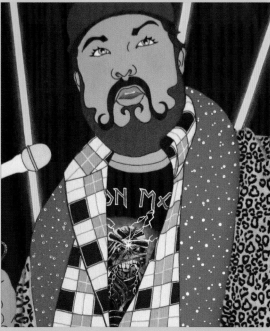

James Gobel, *The Fitting No. 1*, 2007 (detail of p. 41).

James Gobel, *I'll Be Your Friend, I'll Be Your Love, I'll Be Everything You Need*, 2009 (detail of p. 48).

Takashi Murakami, *Eye Love SUPERFLAT*, 2004 (see also p. 53).

Mark Bradford, *Miss China Silk*, 2005 (detail of p. 64).

generated animation) and manga (comics). Japan's major economic and social growth spurt, which began in the 1960s and was in part linked with the post-World War II American investment in its former enemy's economic recovery, stimulated a need for the visual representation of a new society. Japanese anime and manga answered this need and have since invaded the global market, appealing to Eastern and Western audiences alike.

Murakami has sought to draw attention to the dominance of the mass media by creating his own popular-culture brand incorporating anime-inspired characters and design motifs. Embracing what he views as an emptiness in Japanese popular culture, Murakami describes his work as "superflat." This term refers to the compression and two-dimensionality of both anime and traditional Japanese art forms such as woodblock prints, as well as Japan's voracious consumer appetite.

Murakami has exploited the commercial appeal of his art and its overflow into the fashion world. In 2003, he masterminded a brilliant fusion of Japanese pop and elite Western style when he reinterpreted the staid logo of the French luxury leather goods brand Louis Vuitton.[15] Murakami's new logo pattern, which was adapted for a line of handbags, incorporated the bright colors of anime along with his signature "jellyfish eyes," embodying the cheerful yet vacant tone of his art. His successful penetration of Louis Vuitton's ultra-refined image also led to a series of paintings featuring the retooled Louis Vuitton logo on black or white grounds, all titled *Eye Love SUPERFLAT*. These paintings embody East and West, art and commerce, high art and popular culture.

East and West also meet in Mark Bradford's *Miss China Silk*. In this work Bradford portrays the intersection of Chinese and African-American cultures in his hometown of Los Angeles by making explicit African-American women's use of Asian women's hair for weaves. Bradford contemplates the social importance of beauty salon culture among working-class African-American women in urban Los Angeles, where hairstyle is central to black female identity. In Asia meanwhile, women grow and cut their hair to meet the demand among American women for long, straight hair that can be easily styled and dyed. In *Miss China Silk*, Bradford photographs Asian women (his friends) draped in Asian- and African-patterned silks while wearing African-American style hair extensions. Bradford alludes to the connection between Chinese and African-American

17

Raphael, *The Three Graces*, c. 1500–1501. Oil on panel, 6 11/16 x 6 11/16 in. Musée Condé, Chantilly, France.

Yinka Shonibare, *Three Graces*, 2001 (see also p. 43).

Brian Jungen, *Blanket no. 6*, 2008 (detail of p. 56).

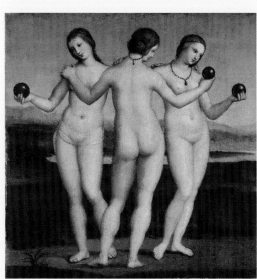

cultures both within urban Los Angeles and on either side of the Pacific.

Yinka Shonibare's art reflects his hybrid Nigerian/British identity. Born in England in 1962 but having lived in the Nigerian capital of Lagos from the age of three to sixteen, he considers himself bi-cultural. Shonibare, whose experiences in both Nigeria and England were defined by newly postcolonial relationships, examines the complex links between African and British cultures through Dutch wax print cotton, a fabric with its own multifaceted cultural history. Originally inspired by Indonesian batik designs, which Dutch colonizers brought back to Europe, Dutch wax fabrics were manufactured and exported by the British to West Africa, where the designs became so popular that by the mid-1960s, they had ironically come to be associated with African identity.[16]

Shonibare's life-size, headless figures often parody an artwork or societal situation that exemplifies the excess and vanity of Victorian, or colonial-era, culture. In *Three Graces* he reinterprets a classical subject, widely portrayed throughout antiquity as well as by the Old Masters and nineteenth-century painters and sculptors. In ancient Greece, the Three Graces were the physical embodiment of charm, beauty, nature, human creativity and fertility.

Lacking the classical elegance and restrained beauty of earlier depictions of the subject, Shonibare's Graces are identifiable only by their title. He based the figures on a nineteenth-century photograph of three women considered models of Victorian virtue. The cultural ambiguity of Shonibare's Graces is marked by their clothing, which is Victorian in style but constructed from Dutch wax print fabric and compounded by their indeterminate race (Shonibare deliberately uses a nondescript color for skin). He taps what may be among the earliest representations of Western standards of beauty and artistic talent to incorporate his own African/British experiences into a dialogue about the very nature of beauty. He communicates the difficulty of straddling cultural traditions whose histories are so intricately yet problematically connected by making it impossible to pinpoint his figures' identities.

A parallel entanglement between two cultures inspired Brian Jungen to tackle the myth of cultural authenticity. Like Yinka Shonibare, Jungen has enjoyed the luxury of moving in and out of his native Dane-zaa Nation in northern British Columbia, where he was raised by a Swiss-Canadian father and First Nations mother.

Exploring the connection of his Dane-zaa heritage to contemporary Western consumer culture, Jungen makes "blankets" inspired by a tradition created to fulfill the uninformed expectations of non-native people. His Blankets appear to be traditionally native but are actually woven from NFL and NBA jerseys, symbols of the very ritualistic, aggressive behavior that Westerners have historically projected onto native groups. Jungen states, "I like to try to pair this idea of ritual and ceremony

Samuel Fosso, *Self-Portrait*, 1977 (detail of p. 49).

Samuel Fosso, *Le Chef*, 1997 (detail of p. 35).

19

in commercial culture with those from more traditional societies."[17] His interweaving of his culture's traditional art forms with objects from consumer culture is not unlike Takashi Murakami's insertion of a Japanese pop aesthetic into another form of Western cultural regalia.

Conflicting cultural expectations also inspired the self-portraits of Samuel Fosso, in which he initially attempted to reconcile contradictory images of masculinity coming from within and penetrating from outside the Central African Republic. Born in Cameroon in 1962, Fosso, like Shonibare, was thrust into an atmosphere of political upheaval following the end of the colonial era. Having made his way to Bangui in the Central African Republic by the age of ten, he apprenticed with a photographer and opened his own portrait studio shortly thereafter. Early in his career as a portrait photographer, Fosso began experimenting with self-portraits after hours in his studio, combining elements of West African portrait photography (African-patterned fabrics for backdrop and costume) with accessories that spoke of Western culture.[18] In his self-portraits, Fosso broke out of the stiffness and formality regularly assumed by sitters in both African and Western portrait photography.

Inspired by images from French magazines, celebrities pictured in newspapers and pictures of popular African and African-American singers, Fosso started out emulating Western disco youth culture. He experimented with theatrical costuming, privately posing in underwear or

tight-fitting clothing, which was not just culturally taboo but forbidden by his government. This was a form of both physical and psychological liberation for Fosso. As he describes, "My work is based on specific situations and people I am familiar with, things I desire, rework in my imagination and then interpret. I borrow an identity…. It's a way of freeing me from myself."[19] Fosso transformed his studio into a space of fantasy and performance in which he staged his own sexuality and celebrity.

Twenty years later, after being discovered by the art world, Fosso was commissioned by the French department store chain Tati to create images for a series of advertisements. He took the opportunity to make a comical yet politically scathing image of an African chief who displays all the traditional regalia but also bears signs of a culture permanently altered by French colonization. Most poignant is the spray of plastic sunflowers that replaces the chief's staff, a primary symbol of his power. Perhaps the flowers symbolize the chief's selling his people out to false promises of wealth and power or his impotence in the face of manipulation by European leaders following colonial occupation.

Shonibare, Bradford, Murakami, Jungen and Fosso all create art that represents not the sum of two cultures but new cultural identities forged through a process of negotiating power and social relationships between conflicting heritages.

Grace Ndiritu, *Still Life:
Lying Down Textiles*,
2005–7 (still from
video installation, see
also p. 63).

Willie Cole, *Procession*,
2006 (detail of p. 52).

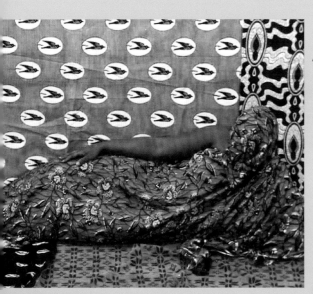

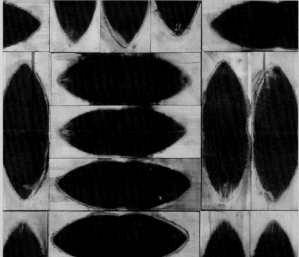

Mapping Cultural Heritage

Artists also use pattern and elements of dress to trace paths through their own cultural ancestry and traditions. Born in London in 1969 to parents of Indian descent, Bharti Kher moved from Britain to New Delhi in 1993. Kher uses the evolution of the bindi, traditionally a red circle painted on the foreheads of married women, to illustrate her own journey of physical and cultural reorientation against the backdrop of India on the cusp of globalization.[20]

Kher applies sticker bindis to the entire surface of a painting to create maplike landscapes that resemble satellite images, stars or migration patterns. Poetic titles like *Mother of anything possible, anytime* echo grand planetary events such as ocean tides, changing seasons and shifting winds (p. 54). Poet and art critic Ranjit Hoskote describes Kher's bindi works as picturing the psychological space of migrants, refugees and nomads. He states, "We no longer move to unexplored new worlds so much as we create new mental…worlds from the environments in which we find ourselves." He refers to Kher, who confronts the intellectual and emotional tumult of displacement as a "strategist of belonging."[21]

The integration of artistic traditions into the everyday life of many non-Western cultures inspired Grace Ndiritu, who is of Kenyan heritage and lives in London, to use textiles as a second skin, mapping her own body in what she calls "handcrafted videos." In the four-screen video projection *Still Life*, Ndiritu is wrapped in or covered by fabrics from Mali. Within a fixed frame, she slowly and seductively caresses her skin and the fabric, appearing and disappearing behind it like a veil. Allowing only the cloth and her skin to identify her, Ndiritu merges her body with the fabric so that the patterns represent her.

Ndiritu cites the 2005 exhibition *Matisse: The Fabric of Dreams, His Art and His Textiles,* which highlighted Matisse's passion for North African, African and Polynesian textiles, as a major source of inspiration for *Still Life* (see Matisse, *The Pink Studio,* p. 14).[22] But rather than place herself within a set of patterned textiles, she becomes intermingled with it. And unlike Matisse, Ndiritu is both the author and the subject of her images, so she controls the viewer's experience of her body. The title *Still Life,* which typically refers to compositions of inanimate objects, contradicts her moving, breathing, undulating body.

Willie Cole's iron-scorched surfaces chart the African diaspora and the experiences of African-American people. Cole, who is primarily influenced by African art, has also derived profound inspiration from steam irons throughout his career. While growing up, he was frequently asked to fix irons for his grandmother and great grandmother, who were both housekeepers. Long fascinated with black and African history, Cole has used irons as an artistic tool through which to explore his experiences as a human being and an African-American man. Steam irons can suggest domestic labor, but as Cole has illustrated, they can also represent a head, a crowded slave ship or a house, depending on their orientation.

In both *Procession* and *Garden,* Cole makes repeated scorch marks on a surface, a practice that evokes flesh branding during the slave trade as well as scarification, tattooing and other beautification practices of various African ethnicities. The designs created by the scorch marks are reminiscent of Yoruba dyed-cloth patterns and imprinted Ashanti Adinkra cloth made in Ghana.[23]

Cole uses the iron to evoke an array of cultural practices that engage textiles as well as human skin, stating, "I want my artworks to be links between worlds." His art specifically tracks the African diaspora, but for him it represents the interconnectedness of all communities, families and cultures. He claims, "My work is not about race. It's about spirit."[24]

Conjuring Utopias

Is "racelessness" a form of a paradise? Japanese artist Aya Uekawa's ambiguously multiracial figures convey what she considers to be her "cultural appearance" rather than her physical likeness. She considers the notion of the exotic from her vantage point inhabiting both Japanese and American cultures. Not unlike Lalla Essaydi and Bharti Kher, Uekawa addresses in her art the struggle to find a sense of belonging amid feelings of alienation both in her native Japan and her new home in New York.

According to the artist, the women depicted in her series Team Player Candidates try but cannot fit into society. She hints at specific periods or cultures through elements of dress and pattern, facial features and hair but offsets them with confounding details. Each of the figures in these paintings has an exaggeratedly long neck evoking Italian Mannerist painting as well as African and Southeast Asian traditions of elongating the neck by wearing stacked coiled necklaces. Each figure's attribute—feathers, charms or pearls—also has cultural associations ranging from purity, wealth and beauty to freedom and status. Uekawa's women represent far-away exoticism or familiar traditions, depending on one's perspective. By combining such diverse physical aspects, artistic styles and details, Uekawa avoids embracing a specific culture.

If Uekawa promotes an absence of race, Nick Cave manifests his utopian vision by gathering together elements of diverse races and cultures. Made of handmade fabrics, beads and sequins collected from thrift stores as well as other salvaged materials such as bottle caps, sticks and hair, Cave's Soundsuits and Tondos project and embody religious, ritualistic and ceremonial traditions from around the world.

The Soundsuits are reminiscent of various African and South American masking traditions in which the wearer's identity is subsumed by the spirit channeled through the performance or "dance" of a specific mask. Although the function and cultural origins of Cave's Soundsuits are ambiguous, he embraces the fact that, like the masks, they similarly obscure their wearers' identities. Museum director Kate Eilertsen describes them as a search for an understanding of identity.[25] A gay African-American man, Cave finds the ability to escape and inhabit different selves liberating. "Refusing to be pinned down to any one...demographic at the expense of another," curator Dan Cameron explains, "enables Cave to behave as a kind of shaman to all people at all times."[26]

Cave views himself as a humanitarian using art as a vehicle to break through racial, ethnic, religious and other barriers. He fantasizes about the role his art might play in our global community, wishing for it to stimulate hope, inspiration and empowerment: "What can I do to spark [people's] dreams? What can I do that will help them remember people and images from their past?" He concludes, "If I can create an opportunity to bring people of all creeds, identities and interests together, then I am doing my work." Not only does Cave wish to spark a collective memory, but his utopia is a place where everyone can freely try on and borrow elements of identity from any cultural heritage.[27]

Aya Uekawa, *A Team Player Candidate (The Chicken Feather)*, 2005 (see also pp. 57 and 62).

Nick Cave, *Soundsuit*, 2009 (detail of p. 51, see also p. 44).

New Notions of Beauty

The artists in *Pattern ID* illustrate the possibility of accumulating and displaying numerous cultural identities at once. They assert beauty in co-existing, contradictory influences and promote a recalibration of aesthetic values in the West toward pluralism. The question of why so many artists today are engaging in such explorations of identity is clearly linked to the heretofore unprecedented accessibility and awareness of cultures brought about by our globalized world. Not only are people more mobile, but the profound interconnectedness and interdependence among world cultures and races can no longer be denied. As the art world has radically expanded in the last two decades to keep pace with global cultural phenomena, artists from around the world have found a voice on the international stage. These artists have often invoked the cultural currency of pattern and dress as crucial elements of their own artistic traditions. Just as cultural boundaries have been blurred, so have artistic categories begun to overlap. Artists are incorporating fashion, design and craft into traditional modes of fine art.

Nearly all the works in *Pattern ID* engage in dialogue with Western art history and notions of ethnography by bringing non-Western influences into the framework of Western art practice. The resulting artwork has permanently expanded our view of cultural relationships through the prism of art history. We can no longer look at a Matisse without thinking of Mickalene Thomas and Grace Ndiritu or at a portrait by Gainsborough without thinking of Kehinde Wiley and Yinka Shonibare. These contemporary artists' personal journeys yield endless future possibilities for the creation of new identities that cannot be located in a physical place but rather reflect, as Nick Cave invokes, the re-ignition of a collective cultural memory. Their work is not just a discourse between cultures, but a discourse on the meaning of culture.

Notes

1 Many Anatolian carpet styles are traditionally named after the European painters who depicted them. *The Ambassadors* gave rise to the pattern name for this style of carpet: large-pattern Holbein, which is characterized by several large geometric motifs with interlacing or strapwork surrounded by smaller motifs in the field and borders. Knotted pile carpets like this one were produced in commercial workshops in Anatolia for sale within the Islamic world and for export to Europe. In the Islamic world they were used as floor coverings, but in Europe they were used on tables and benches because of their high cost. See Walter B. Denny, *The Classical Tradition in Anatolian Carpets* (Washington, D.C., and London: Textile Museum and Scala Publishers Ltd., 2002).

The green textile in the background is a silk damask with a so-called pomegranate pattern. This pattern is characterized by floral and foliate motifs arranged in an ogival lattice, and derives from Persian sources via the Ottoman Empire into Italy and the rest of Europe. In the early sixteenth century, silks of this type were almost certainly Italian (from Venice or Genoa) but could possibly have been woven in Spain. My thanks to Cecilia Anderson for this information.

2 Roger Benjamin, *Orientalist Aesthetics: Art, Colonialism, and French North Africa, 1880–1930* (Berkeley: University of California Press, 2003), 175. For more on Matisse and his use of textiles, see Ann Dumas and Norman Rosenthal, *Matisse, His Art and His Textiles: The Fabric of Dreams* (London: Royal Academy of Arts, 2004).

3 Lalla Essaydi, *Converging Territories* (New York: PowerHouse Books, 2005), 28.

4 Homi Bhabha, in Brian Jungen, *Brian Jungen* (Rotterdam: Witte de With Center for Contemporary Art, 2006), 15.

5 Numerous authors have written about the relationship between dress (which includes garments, hair, cosmetics, jewelry, etc.) and identity. For further reading, see Eugenia Paulicelli and Hazel Clark, ed., *The Fabric of Cultures: Fashion, Identity, and Globalization* (New York: Routledge, 2009), or Mary Ellen Roach-Higgins, *Dress and Identity* (New York: Fairchild Publications, 1995).

6 David Keeps, "Wiley World," *Advocate* (June–July 2009), 107–9.

7 Joe Wood, "The Yellow Negro," *Transition*, no. 73 (1997), 40–66.

8 During the Edo period of imperial rule, the shogunate placed sanctions on Japanese citizens that limited everything from expenditure of money to modes of dress. Set apart from the city, the floating world had no such sanctions; courtesans could be freely had, with music, theater and other forms of physical and intellectual pleasures on offer.

9 Although Wiley allows his subjects to choose a pose, he guides them in creating the composition he desires.

10 In her exhibition catalog *Black Male,* Thelma Golden charts the societal representation of the black male body since the 1960s, citing the many problematic stereotypes that still pervade our culture. For further reading see Golden, *Black Male: Representations of Masculinity in Contemporary American Art* (New York: Whitney Museum of American Art, 1995).

11 Emil Wilbekin, "Master Class," in *Kehinde Wiley: Columbus* (Columbus: Columbus Museum of Art, 2006), 28.

12 In his *The Question of Lay Analysis* (1926), Freud referred to female sexuality as "a dark continent," equating it with African explorer John Rowlands Stanley's description of exploring a dark forest—virgin, hostile, impenetrable. Equating women's sexuality with "Africa" served to amplify the fear of African women's sexuality.

13 Essaydi, *Converging Territories,* 28.

14 The title plays on the lyrics to the Communards' 1986 song "Disenchanted."

15 Murakami collaborated on the handbags with Marc Jacobs, then creative director for Louis Vuitton. In an era when luxury brands that have traditionally stood for the old European elite have been extensively co-opted by the nouveau riche to broadcast their status, many brands such as Louis Vuitton now have dual identities, launching diverging advertising campaigns with spokespeople ranging from hip-hop star Pharell to former 007 Sean Connery.

16 For a more in-depth explanation of the origins of Dutch wax-printed cotton, see Cecilia Gunzburger Anderson, "We Are What We Wear: Cross-Cultural Uses of Textiles," p.

70 in this catalog. For further reading on the topic, see Robert Hobbs, "Yinka Shonibare MBE: The Politics of Representation," 24–35, in Yinka Shonibare, *Yinka Shonibare, MBE* (Munich; New York: Prestel, 2008), or John Picton, "Laughing at Ourselves" in *Yinka Shonibare: Double Dutch* (Rotterdam: Museum Boijmans Van Beuningen; Vienna: Kunsthalle Wien; Rotterdam, NAi Publishers, 2004), 45–62.

17 Jessica Morgan, "Out of Bounds: Brian Jungen," Qvest.com, 2008, http://91.186.11.41/qvest/home/art/ggbrian-jungen (accessed May 11, 2009).

18 Fosso's predecessor Seydou Keïta (1921–2001) gained international renown for his striking portraits in which the sitters often wore lush printed fabrics that were combined with patterned backdrops and paired with Western props. Keïta worked in Bamako, Mali, in the 1950s and 1960s. Malick Sidibé, also working in Bamako, documented youth culture in the 1950s through 1970s. His portraits similarly feature multiple patterned fabrics and Western fashions.

19 Guido Schlinkert, "Transformer," in *Samuel Fosso* (Milan: 5 Continents Editions, 2006), 25.

20 Traditionally worn only by married Hindu women in India, bindis are now worn by other women, too. Decorative sticker bindis are available in all sizes and colors and are worn as a fashion statement by women of every age, marital status and religion.

21 Ranjit Hoskote, *The Pursuit of Extreme Propositions: Recent Works by Bharti Kher* (New York: Jack Shainman Gallery, 2009), 16–17.

22 The exhibition was organized by the Metropolitan Museum of Art, New York; the Royal Academy of Arts, London; and Le Musée Matisse, Le Cateau-Cambrésis.

23 For further discussion on connections between Cole's scorch-marked works and Ghanaian textiles, see Anderson, "We Are What We Wear," p. 72.

24 Patterson Sims, *Anxious Objects: Willie Cole's Favorite Brands* (New Brunswick, N.J.: Rutgers University Press, 2006), 96.

25 Kate Eilertsen, introduction to *Nick Cave: Meet Me at the Center of the Earth* (San Francisco: Yerba Buena Center for the Arts, 2009), 18.

26 Dan Cameron, "Shape Shifting," in ibid., 22.

27 Nick Cave and Kate Eilersten, "Working Toward What I Am Leaving Behind," in ibid., 231.

ARTIST BIOGRAPHIES

Mark Bradford

Born in Los Angeles, 1961
Lives and works in Los Angeles

A formerly self-described "beauty operator," Mark Bradford was in charge of painting signs for his mother's hair salon as a teenager. He draws inspiration from his working-class background as well as the diverse cultural makeup of his southern California community. Bradford received both his MFA (1997) and BFA (1995) from the California Institute of the Arts in Valencia. His work has been included in exhibitions at the Los Angeles County Museum of Art (2006), the New Museum, New York (2007), the Walker Art Center, Minneapolis (2007), and the Hammer Museum, Los Angeles (2007). Bradford had a solo exhibition at the Whitney Museum of American Art, New York (2003), and he has a solo exhibition scheduled at the Wexner Center for the Arts, Columbus, Ohio, in 2010. Bradford was the 2006 recipient of the Bucksbaum Award, a 2003 recipient of a Louis Comfort Tiffany Foundation grant and a 2002 recipient of a Joan Mitchell Foundation grant. Bradford is a recipient of a 2009 MacArthur Fellow award.

iona rozeal brown

Born in Washington, D.C., 1966
Lives and works in Washington, D.C.

As a child, iona rozeal brown was drawn to Asian cultures and encouraged by her parents to have Asian friends. Moved by writer Joe Wood's 1997 article "The Yellow Negro" in which he discussed *ganguro*, a group of Japanese youth that adopted American hip-hop style and culture, brown traveled to Japan to meet ganguro kids. She visited Japan again in 2005 to study Kabuki theater. She received her MFA from the Yale University School of Art (2002) and her BFA from the San Francisco Art Institute (1999). brown's work has been included in group exhibitions at the Museum of the African Diaspora, San Francisco (2005), and the High Museum of Art, Atlanta (2006). She has solo exhibitions scheduled at the Museum of Contemporary Art Cleveland and the Museum of Contemporary Art Detroit in 2010. brown was a 2007 recipient of a Joan Mitchell Foundation grant and a Louis Comfort Tiffany Foundation grant.

Nick Cave

Born in Jefferson City, Missouri, 1959
Lives and works in Chicago

Nick Cave became interested in fashion while attempting to make hand-me-downs from his six older brothers "his own." Along with his penchant for fashion, Cave sought self-expression through dance and trained with the Alvin Ailey American Dance Theater. As a gay African-American male, he has sometimes felt devalued by society and found comfort in the sense of transformation through dance and fashion. Cave is currently an associate professor and chairman of the Fashion Department of the School of the Art Institute of Chicago. He received his MFA from the Cranbrook Academy of Art, Bloomfield Hills, Michigan (1989) and his BFA from the Kansas City Art Institute, Missouri (1982). He has had solo exhibitions at the Allentown Art Museum, Pennsylvania (2002), the Chicago Cultural Center (2006), the Museum of Contemporary Art Jacksonville (2008), as well as a mid-career survey at the Yerba Buena Center for the Arts, San Francisco (2009). He has a solo exhibition scheduled at Studio La Città, Verona, Italy, in 2010. Cave was a recipient of a 2001 Louis Comfort Tiffany Foundation grant and a 2008 Joan Mitchell Foundation grant.

Willie Cole

Born in Somerville, New Jersey, 1955
Lives and works in Mine Hill, New Jersey

After his parents divorced, Willie Cole grew up in an all-female household with his grandmother, mother and sister. As the "man of the house," he was frequently called upon to fix things, including irons, to which he developed a lifelong attraction. Frequently finding discarded irons on the street, he began accumulating them in his early teens. Cole also had a childhood fascination with Africa, which drove his later interest in African art forms. Cole studied art, theater and music, and he majored in fashion design at Arts High School, Newark, New Jersey. He attended the Art Students League, New York (1976–79) and received his BFA from the School of Visual Arts, New York (1976). Cole has had solo exhibitions at the Tampa Museum of Art (2004), the Bronx Museum of the Arts (2001), the Miami Art Museum, Florida (2000), the Museum of Modern Art, New York (1998), and a collaborative exhibition at the Amistad Center for Art & Culture, Hartford, Connecticut (2009). Cole was the recipient of a 1995 Louis Comfort Tiffany Foundation grant and a 1996 Joan Mitchell Foundation grant.

Lalla Essaydi

Born in Marrakesh, Morocco, 1956
Lives and works in New York City and Morocco

Having lived in Saudi Arabia and the United States in addition to her native Morocco, Lalla Essaydi has encountered vastly differing experiences as a female in society. The large, unoccupied house in which Essaydi makes her photographs was her childhood home. Revisiting this space has provided her the opportunity to examine the evolution of her identity as a Muslim woman. Essaydi received her MFA from the School of the Museum of Fine Arts, Boston (2003) and her BFA from Tufts University, Medford, Massachusetts (1999). She has had solo exhibitions at DeCordova Sculpture Park and Museum, Lincoln, Massachusetts (2009), the New Britain Museum of American Art, Connecticut (2006), the Williams College Museum of Art, Williamstown, Massachusetts (2006), and the Columbus Museum of Art, Ohio (2005). Essaydi has a solo exhibition scheduled at the North Carolina Museum of Art in 2010.

Samuel Fosso

Born in Kumba, Cameroon, 1962
Lives and works in Bangui, Central African Republic

Samuel Fosso spent the first four years of his life unable to move his arms or legs. His mysterious paralysis was cured by his grandfather, the village chief and healer. Having lived in Nigeria from 1965 to 1972, Fosso fled the country in the wake of the Biafran War with his uncle and settled in Bangui, the capital of the Central African Republic. He opened his own photography studio at the age of thirteen and three years later began making self-portraits to send to his grandmother. Fosso's work has been included in numerous group exhibitions including the Centre Pompidou, Paris (2005), the Museum of Contemporary Art, Sydney (2006), and the Studio Museum Harlem, New York (2004). He had a solo exhibition at the Calcografia, Rome (2004). Fosso was the recipient of the Akron Art Museum 2006 Knight Purchase Award for Photographic Media.

James Gobel

Born in Portland, Oregon, 1972
Lives and works in San Francisco

At age fifteen James Gobel moved to Las Vegas and instantly fell in love with its lights and neon. He frequently used glitter in his early paintings to celebrate the city's luminosity. Gobel eventually began using felt and yarn, the highly tactile media that he works with today. Gobel received his MFA from the University of California, Santa Barbara (1999) and his BFA from the University of Nevada, Las Vegas (1996). He has been included in group exhibitions at the Las Vegas Art Museum (2007), Art Rotterdam, the Netherlands (2005), and the New Museum, New York (2005). Gobel had solo exhibitions at the Hammer Museum, Los Angeles and the Contemporary Arts Forum, Santa Barbara (2000).

Brian Jungen

Born in Fort St. John, British Columbia, 1970
Lives and works in Vancouver, British Columbia

Born in a remote logging town in what is commonly referred to as the "interior," Brian Jungen recalls a childhood tension between his awareness of being secluded and his exposure to the larger world via television, which led to his interest in looking at how his aboriginal heritage has been manipulated by global capitalism. Jungen graduated from the Emily Carr Institute of Art + Design, Vancouver, British Columbia (1992) and has had solo exhibitions at the National Museum of the American Indian, Smithsonian Institution, Washington, D.C. (2009), the Tate Modern, London (2006), the Musée d'art contemporain de Montréal (2006), and the New Museum, New York (2005).

Bharti Kher

Born in London, 1969
Lives and works in New Delhi

Born to Indian parents, Bharti Kher moved from her home in London to New Delhi in 1993. Kher used this experience of displacement to both observe contemporary Indian life and explore her own Indian identity. Kher received her BA at the Foundation Course in Art and Design Newcastle Polytechnic, New Castle, England (1991). Her work has been included in exhibitions at the Nerman Museum of Contemporary Art, Overland Park, Kansas (2008), the Serpentine Gallery, London (2008), the South African National Gallery, Cape Town (2007), and the Prince of Wales Museum of Western India (2002), among others. Kher had a solo exhibition at the Baltic Centre for Contemporary Art, Gateshead, England (2008).

Takashi Murakami

Born in Tokyo, 1962
Lives and works in Tokyo

An avid student of contemporary Japanese society, Takashi Murakami draws inspiration from the pervasive presence of anime, comics and video games in Japanese popular culture. Embracing the capitalistic machine of the art market, in 1996 Murakami began Kaikai Kiki Co. Ltd., an art production company and artist management organization. He earned his PhD (1993), MFA (1988) and BFA (1986) from the Tokyo National University of Fine Arts and Music. Murakami has had solo exhibitions at the Fondation Cartier, Paris (2002), the Museum of Contemporary Art Tokyo (2001), the Museum of Fine Arts, Boston (2001), as well as a retrospective organized by the Museum of Contemporary Art, Los Angeles (2007).

Grace Ndiritu

Born in Birmingham, England, 1976
Lives and works in London

Grace Ndiritu grew up surrounded by African textiles and around age seven began taking these fabrics to school to make clothes for her friends on the playground. As an adult, her interest in fabrics as a vehicle for creative expression deepened following journeys to the Himalayas, Iceland, India, Mali and beyond. Ndiritu studied textile art at the Winchester School of Art in England and video art at De Ateliers in Amsterdam. Her work has been included in group exhibitions at the Tate Britain, London (2009), the Studio Museum Harlem, New York (2008), the Dakar Biennale, Senegal (2008), and the Metropolitan Museum of Art, New York (2008).

Yinka Shonibare, MBE

Born in London, 1962
Lives and works in London

At age three, Yinka Shonibare's Nigerian parents returned to their native Lagos and established a home in which British and African cultures coexisted. Although Shonibare attended an elite English-speaking school in Lagos, he was encouraged to speak Yoruba at home. The role clothing plays in conveying cultural identity was impressed upon him at an early age when his father, a successful lawyer, left for work donning a European-style suit yet wore African robes at home. Shonibare attended Byam Shaw School of Art, London (1984–89) and Goldsmiths College, London (1989–91). He has had solo exhibitions at the Speed Art Museum, Louisville (2006), the Miami Art Museum, Florida (2008), the Santa Barbara Museum of Art (2009), as well as a traveling retrospective organized by the Museum of Contemporary Art, Sydney (2008). Shonibare has a solo exhibition scheduled at the Museum of Fine Arts, Boston in 2010. He is the 2010 recipient of the Fourth Plinth Commission in Trafalgar Square. In 2005 Shonibare was designated a Member of the Order of the British Empire (MBE), a British order of chivalry, which he ironically embraces given that his work promotes the ambiguity of his hybrid African/British identity.

29

Mickalene Thomas

Born in Camden, New Jersey, 1971
Lives and works in New York City

Mickalene Thomas is inspired by such diverse influences as Henri Matisse, West African portrait photography and the interior decorations and popular culture of the 1970s. Thomas blends these aesthetic threads as a way of reconstituting her personal experiences. She views the women in her works—African-American women who exude a self-possessed beauty and eroticism—as extensions of herself. Thomas received her MFA from the Yale University School of Art (2002) and her BFA from the Pratt Institute, Brooklyn, New York (2000). She has had solo exhibitions at the Indianapolis Museum of Contemporary Art (2007), the Santa Barbara Contemporary Arts Forum (2008) and La Conservera Contemporary Art Space, Ceuti, Spain (2009). Thomas was a 2007 recipient of a Rema Hort Mann Foundation grant.

Aya Uekawa

Born in Tokyo, 1979
Lives and works in Beacon, New York

As a child in Japan, Aya Uekawa attended strict schools whose stringent codes of behavior and dress stifled her self-expression. Uekawa cites her experience of growing up under such conditions as a cause for her difficulty adjusting to life in New York City and her propensity to repeat the same forms and patterns in her work. She received her MFA (2008) and BFA (2004) from Hunter College of the City University of New York. Uekawa had a solo exhibition at the Contemporary Arts Center in Cincinnati (2009).

Kehinde Wiley

Born in Los Angeles, 1977
Lives and works in New York City

Kehinde Wiley was raised by a single mother in South Central Los Angeles. As a child, he ran a "junk store," selling used faux French furniture, old clothing and paintings. He enjoyed the opportunity this enterprise afforded him to interact with his neighbors, and the objects he pedaled helped establish his flamboyant, decorative aesthetic. At age twenty, Wiley flew to Africa to meet his Nigerian father for the first time. Wiley received his MFA from the Yale University School of Art (2001) and his BFA from the San Francisco Art Institute (1999). His work has been included in group exhibitions at institutions such as the National Portrait Gallery, Smithsonian Institution, Washington, D.C. (2008) and the Whitney Museum of American Art, New York (2006). He has had solo exhibitions at the Portland Art Museum, Oregon (2007), the Columbus Museum of Art, Ohio (2006) and the Brooklyn Museum of Art (2004). Wiley has a solo exhibition scheduled at the Museu de Arte Moderna, Rio de Janeiro in 2010. Wiley was the recipient of a 2002 Rema Hort Mann Foundation grant and a 2008 Americans for the Arts Young Artist Award for Artistic Excellence.

WORKS IN THE EXHIBITION

32

Lalla Essaydi
Converging Territories #31,
2003
Chromogenic print
mounted to aluminum
48 x 60 in.
Courtesy Edwynn Houk
Gallery, New York

Mickalene Thomas
Girlfriends and Lovers, 2008
Rhinestones, acrylic and
enamel on wood panel
108 x 144 in.
Collection of the Akron Art
Museum, The Mary S. and
Louis S. Myers Endowment
Fund for Painting
and Sculpture 2010.1

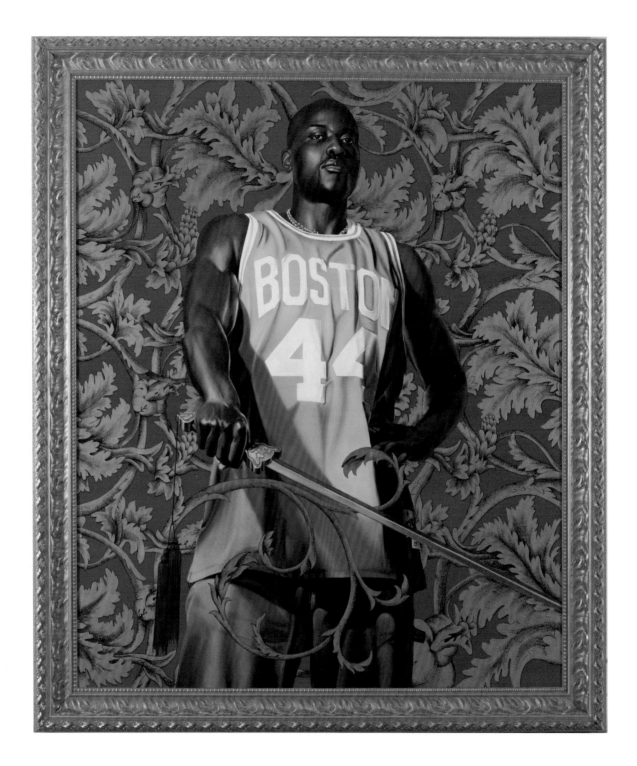

34

Kehinde Wiley
Alexander the Great,
2007
Oil and enamel
on canvas
72 x 60 in.
Ann and Mel Schaffer
Family Collection

Samuel Fosso
Le Chef [The Chief], 1997
Chromogenic print
20 x 20 in.
Collection of the Akron
Art Museum, Knight
Purchase Fund for
Photographic Media
2009.26

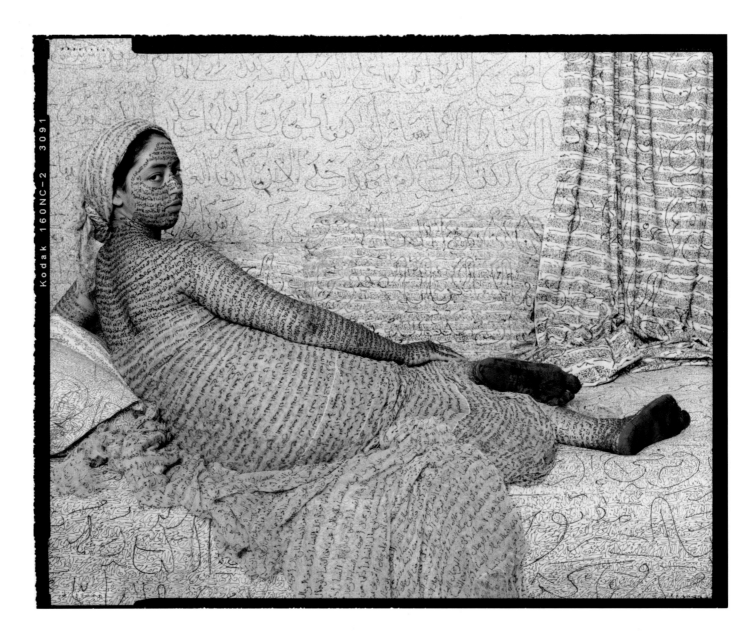

Lalla Essaydi
Les Femmes du Maroc:
Grande Odalisque, 2008
Chromogenic print
mounted to aluminum
48 x 60 in.
Courtesy Edwynn Houk
Gallery, New York

iona rozeal brown
Introducing: Kaatchi the surrogate, and *Introducing: Kenna the siren, polyphony in G with moorfish,* 2008
Mixed media on panel (diptych)
52 x 38 in. each panel
Collection of David A. Sachs and Karen Richards Sachs

38

Nick Cave
Tondo, 2009
Appliquéd found beaded
and sequined garments
96 in. diameter
Courtesy the artist and
Jack Shainman Gallery,
New York

Mickalene Thomas
A Moments Pleasure #2,
2008
Rhinestones, acrylic and
enamel on wood panel
72 x 84 in.
Collection of
Christopher Melton

Samuel Fosso
*La Femme libérée américaine
dans les années 70
[Liberated American
Woman in the 70s]*, 1997
Chromogenic print
20 x 20 in.
Collection of the Akron
Art Museum, Knight Purchase
Fund for Photographic Media
2006.26

James Gobel
The Fitting No. 2, 2007
Felt, yarn and
acrylic on canvas
46 x 30 in.
Courtesy Kravets/
Wehby, New York

The Fitting No. 1, 2007
Felt, yarn and
acrylic on canvas
84 x 72 in.
Courtesy Kravets/
Wehby, New York

42

Willie Cole
Garden (Ozone Summer Series), 1991
Scorch marks on canvas
94 x 48 in.
Collection of the
Progressive Corporation,
Cleveland, Ohio

Yinka Shonibare, MBE
Three Graces, 2001
Three life-size fiberglass
mannequins, Dutch wax
print cotton
Collection of The Speed
Art Museum, Louisville,
Kentucky, purchased
with funds from
the Alice Speed Stoll
Accessions Trust

Nick Cave
Soundsuit, 2009
Found crocheted hats
and bags, appliqué
and knitted yarn
100 x 42 x 32 in.
Courtesy the artist
and Jack Shainman
Gallery, New York

Soundsuit, 2009
Fabric with appliquéd
crochet and buttons,
knitted yarn and metal
armature
97 x 26 x 20 in.
Courtesy the artist
and Jack Shainman
Gallery, New York

Lalla Essaydi
Les Femmes du Maroc
#26A, 2006
Chromogenic print
mounted to aluminum
60 x 48 in.
Courtesy Edwynn Houk
Gallery, New York

46

Mickalene Thomas
It Hurts So Good!
(Brawlin' Spitfire Two), 2007

Brian Jungen
Blanket no. 4, 2008
Hand-woven professional
sports jerseys
51 1/2 x 51 1/4 in.
Courtesy the artist and
Casey Kaplan, New York

48

James Gobel
I'll Be Your Friend, I'll Be Your Love, I'll Be Everything You Need, 2009
Felt, yarn, acrylic and rhinestones on canvas
72 x 56 in.
Collection of the Akron Art Museum, Purchased with funds from the Gay Community Endowment Fund of Akron Community Foundation, Steven P. Schmidt and Richard J. Krochka, and Museum Acquisition Fund   2010.43

Samuel Fosso
Self-Portrait, 1977
Gelatin silver print
20 x 20 in.
Collection of the Akron
Art Museum, Knight
Purchase Fund for
Photographic Media,
2006.29

Kehinde Wiley
*Santos Dumont—
The Father of Aviation III,*
2009
Oil on canvas
72 x 96 in.
Private collection,
Los Angeles

Nick Cave
Soundsuit, 2009
Metal flowers and
armature, fabric with
appliquéd beading,
sequins and embroidery
111 1/2 x 42 x 32 in.
Courtesy the artist
and Jack Shainman
Gallery, New York

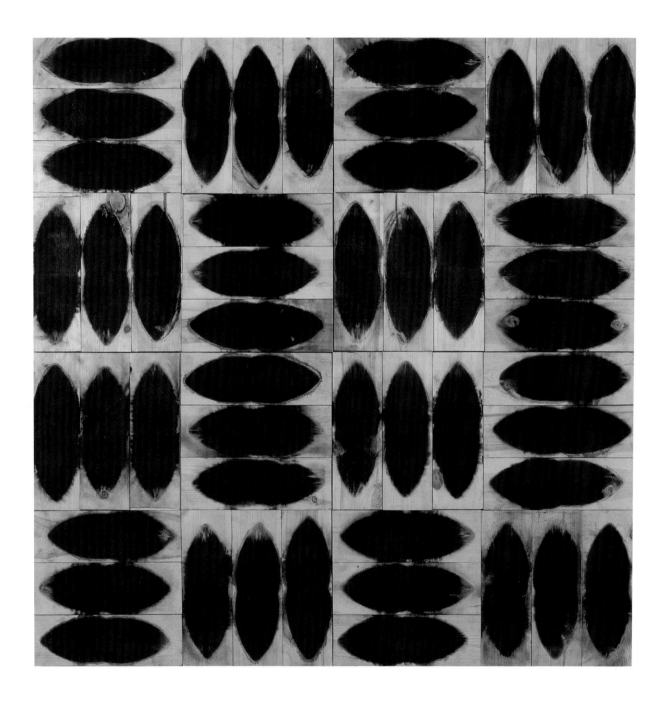

Willie Cole
Procession, 2006
Scorched plywood
66 1/2 x 66 1/2 in.
Courtesy Alexander
and Bonin, New York

Takashi Murakami
Eye Love SUPERFLAT, 2004
Acrylic on canvas
mounted on wood
23 5/8 x 23 5/8 in.
Private collection, New
York, courtesy Marianne
Boesky Gallery, New York

Eye Love SUPERFLAT, 2003
Acrylic on canvas
mounted on wood
23 5/8 x 23 5/8 in.
Private collection,
New York, courtesy
Marianne Boesky Gallery,
New York

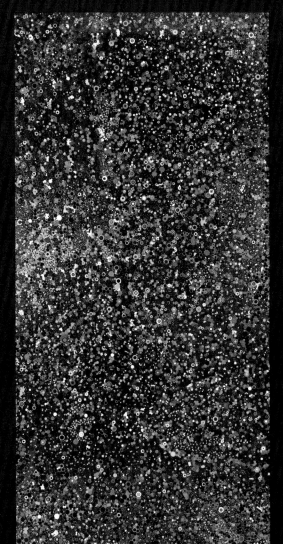
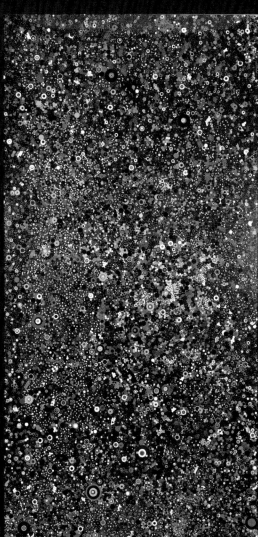
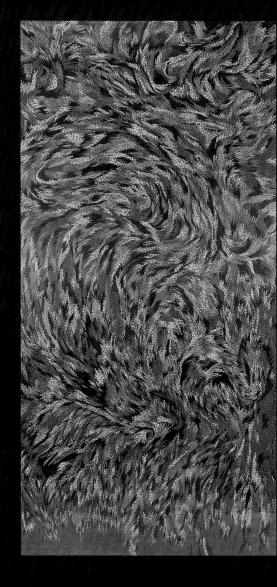

Bharti Kher
Mother of anything possible, anytime, 2006
Bindis on aluminum composite panel (triptych)
96 x 48 in.
each panel
Collection of Ranbir Singh

Yinka Shonibare, MBE
La Méduse, 2008
C-print mounted on aluminum
85 x 107 x 3 1/2 in.
Collection of the Akron Art Museum, Knight Purchase Fund for Photographic Media 2010.2

Brian Jungen
Blanket no. 6, 2008
Hand-woven professional
sports jerseys
50 1/4 x 46 in.
Courtesy the artist and
Casey Kaplan, New York

iona rozeal brown
a3 blackface #55, 2003
53 x 41 in.
Acrylic on paper
Collection of the
Progressive Corporation,
Cleveland, Ohio

Aya Uekawa

A Team Player Candidate (The Chicken Feather), 2004

Acrylic on canvas

22 x 17 in.

Courtesy Kravets/Wehby, New York

Mickalene Thomas

This Is Where I Came In, 2006

Rhinestones, acrylic and enamel on wood panel

72 x 60 in.

Collection of the artist

Kehinde Wiley
*The Dead Christ in
the Tomb,* 2007
Oil and enamel on
canvas
30 x 144 in.
Sender Collection

60

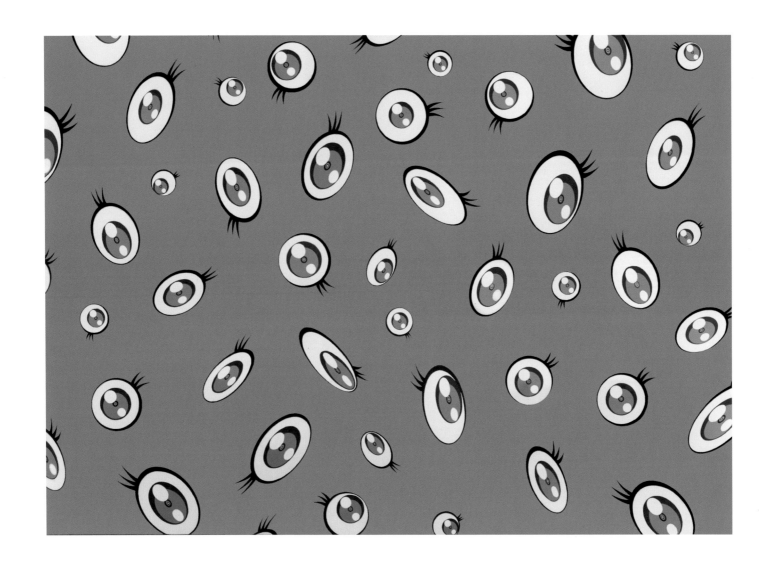

Takashi Murakami
Jellyfish Eyes, 2002
Acrylic on canvas on
board, 28 x 39 in.
Private collection,
Courtesy SHAHEEN
Modern and Contempo-
rary Art, Cleveland

Bharti Kher
Diamonds, 2007
Bindis on painted board
64 1/2 x 70 1/4 in.
Collection of Jack
Shainman and Claude
Simard, New York

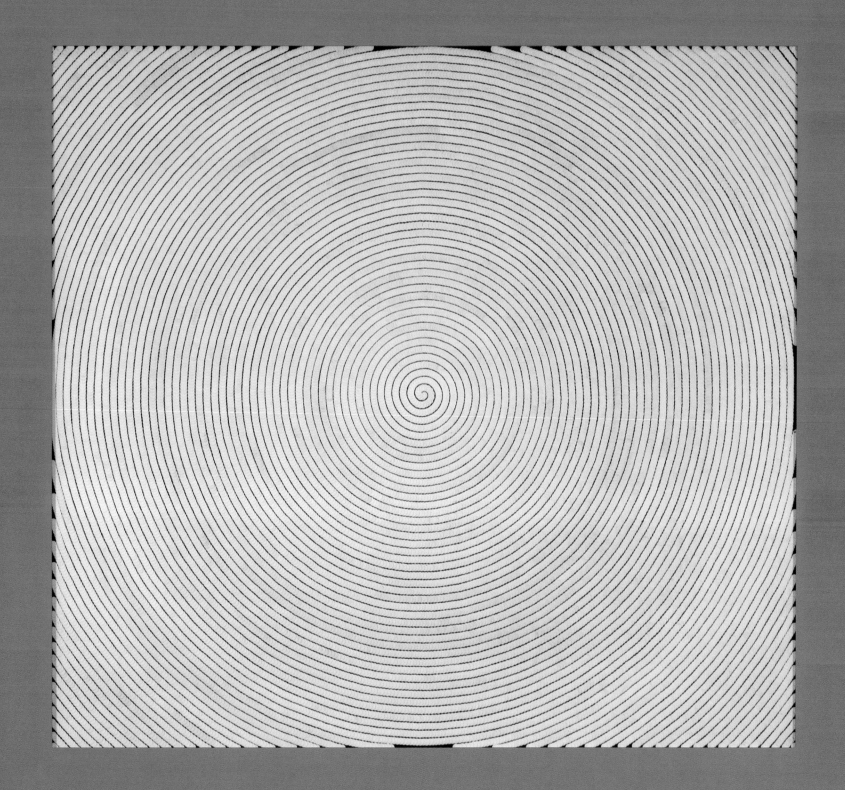

62

Lalla Essaydi
Les Femmes du Maroc:
Moorish Woman, 2008
Chromogenic print
mounted to aluminum
60 x 48 in.
Courtesy Edwynn Houk
Gallery, New York

Aya Uekawa
A Team Player Candidate
(Pearl Necklaces), 2005
Acrylic on canvas
24 x 18 in.
Collection of Stephen
Heighton

Grace Ndiritu
Still Life: White Textiles,
2005–7
From *Still Life*, four-
screen video installation
Courtesy the artist

64

Mark Bradford
Miss China Silk, 2005
Set of 4 C-prints
14 x 11 in. each
Courtesy Sikkema
Jenkins & Co., New York

iona rozeal brown
a3 blackface #67, 2003
Acrylic on paper
50 x 38 in.
Collection of Richard Price

66

Kehinde Wiley
The Blessing Christ,
2007
Oil and enamel
on canvas
72 x 60 in.
Collection of Glenn
Fuhrman New York,
Courtesy the
FLAG Art Foundation

Aya Uekawa
*A Team Player Candidate
(The Charm Lover),* 2005
Acrylic on canvas
28 x 24 in.
Collection of Alison
and Lawrence Wolfson,
New York

WE ARE WHAT WE WEAR:

CROSS-CULTURAL

USES OF TEXTILES

Cecilia Gunzburger Anderson

Textiles are a human constant. Virtually every human society, in every area across the globe and in every era since the Upper Paleolithic, has produced textiles. Cloth surrounds us for most of our lives and beyond, from the newborn baby's swaddling blanket to the clothes we wear every day, from the furnishings that decorate our living spaces to the shroud that encloses us in the grave.

The specific textiles used within a given society reflect multiple influences, including the raw materials available in the local environment; historical, political and religious forces; and contact and trade with others both near and far. As such, textiles are fully intertwined with identity: gender, power, status, life stage, occupation, ethnicity, hometown and other personal attributes are communicated by textiles and clothing.

As trade goods, textiles have a long global history. Wool textiles from the Caucasus from the first millennium BC have been found in China, Chinese silk from 300 BC in Europe and Indian cotton from at least 500 AD in Egypt.[1] The very name of the great Eurasian trade route–the Silk Road–evinces the primacy of textiles among the goods bought and sold from one end of the continent to the other. Textile makers have taken advantage of these trade routes to expand their markets for centuries as well. From the fifth century, Indian dyers commanded a global market, producing designs specific to a variety of markets including Southeast Asia, Europe and Japan, while Chinese workshops produced painted and embroidered textiles for the European market from the seventeenth century.

Textiles were in turn at the forefront of Europe's colonial system. The insect dye cochineal used for Europe's scarlet cloth was the second most valuable export from Spain's American colonies, surpassed only by silver. As the first product of the Industrial Revolution, cloth was traded for furs in North America, gold in West Africa and spices in Southeast Asia.

Foreign textiles acquired through trade have everywhere been transformed by their receivers into meaningful objects on their own cultural terms. Since textiles worn on and displayed around the body are integral in constructing and communicating identity, an imported textile must be made to work within the social mores of its new home. For this reason, textiles are rarely used in the same way in the places they are traded as in their places of origin. In Europe, for example, Chinese silks and Indian chintz were eagerly incorporated into European-style fashionable dress, and their designs were assimilated into locally produced cloth. People in the Americas, Africa and Southeast Asia used the industrially produced cloth they received in trade as a base for their own resist-dyeing or embellishing traditions, and they even unraveled it and rewove the thread into their own types of textiles.

Textiles serve as powerful artifacts for artistic appropriation and manipulation expressly because of the cultural history they bear. The artists in *Pattern ID* use these critical markers of identity to illustrate the breakdown of boundaries historically constructed to divide people into ethnicities, races and classes. As people, goods and

Dutch wax print cloth worn by women in market, Burkina Faso, 1990s.

information travel ever more quickly around the world, textiles paradoxically function both as an immediate visual identifier of a person's origins and as a raw material for constructing a unique personal history.

African Paradoxes

Textiles in West Africa have been important trade goods for as long as records indicate. Among imported textiles, the boldly patterned, brightly colored printed fabric so popular in West Africa known as Dutch wax print is perhaps the most culturally complex. Dutch merchants first encountered wax-resist dyed textiles in the seventeenth century on the Indonesian island of Java and called them by the Malay word *batik*.[2] By the nineteenth century, Dutch textile manufacturers had devised a way to imitate Javanese hand-drawn batik by roller printing a resin resist on the cloth prior to dyeing, which created a distinctive cracked or veined effect in the finished design. Failing to find a market in Indonesia, the Dutch and by then English makers of so-called wax prints instead were surprised to find that West Africans were eager to buy the cloth.

Soon the Dutch and English textile companies abandoned their Indonesian-style designs and began designing specifically for the African market. Motifs representing important African symbols such as stools and staffs appeared, as well as designs based on African proverbs. Ever-cheaper roller-printed versions of the cloth, called fancy prints, were created to capture wider swathes of the market, and when the colonial era ended in the 1960s many African-owned companies began producing these fancy prints. The top-quality and most expensive versions, however, remain those of the Dutch Vlisco Company, whose designers are exclusively European and who call their product "Real Dutch Wax." Bright printed cloths, from Real Dutch Wax to inexpensive African fancy prints, are used ubiquitously in West and Central Africa to make women's clothes in particular, but also to make men's clothes and for every other conceivable use for textiles. What originated as a European imitation of a Southeast Asian textile is now iconic of African culture.

Yinka Shonibare, a British artist of Nigerian descent, uses the immediate association of Dutch wax fabric with Africa to expose the complex nature of identity. By using this colonial commodity in his Victorian-inspired vignettes, Shonibare inserts Africa into the world of European high society and makes explicit the colonial source of Europe's wealth. The colonial economic model involved extracting

raw materials from colonized lands and then selling manufactured goods back to the colony. In *La Méduse*, Shonibare used Dutch wax print cloth for the sails on a ship that carried Europeans to Africa (p. 55). Instead of being stored in the cargo hold awaiting sale to colonial subjects, the fabric has become the physical means of propelling the Europeans; the commodity cloth is literally the engine driving the colonization project.

Shonibare is fully cognizant of the non-African origin of this fabric, calling it "a metaphor…of interdependence,"[3] and he uses its inauthenticity to challenge the idea that identity has fixed boundaries. In Shonibare's meticulous replicas of eighteenth- and nineteenth-century European fashionable dress, the fabrics invite differing interpretations from different viewers. Untrained Western eyes will likely associate the fabric with Africa, but African viewers will notice that Shonibare uses only Real Dutch Wax fabric, the most expensive version made in Holland. This cloth indicates high status in Africa, worn by the same strata of upper-middle-class women as the fashionable Victorian ladies in Shonibare's *Three Graces* (p. 43). African and Western viewers may also notice the sly use of motifs, such as the double-C Chanel logo on one of the Grace's skirts.

Printed fabric also figures prominently in the work of Grace Ndiritu, who is of Kenyan descent but was born and raised in England. In her video performance pieces, the screen is filled with swaths of fabric among which she slowly moves, revealing and concealing her nude limbs with mesmerizing fluidity. As uncut lengths of fabric direct from the bolt, her textiles recall traditional woven African textiles, which are also not cut and tailored into garments, but are worn wrapped or draped around the body. Ndiritu in fact does use African-produced fancy print fabric, made in Mopti, Mali, rather than the Dutch-produced version in Shonibare's work. By choosing the African-printed cloth, Ndiritu fashions herself an African everywoman, draped in the most accessibly priced and therefore most commonly worn version of this type of fabric.

Ndiritu, like Shonibare, often chooses patterns communicative to those in the know: the motif on the white fabric in *Still Life: White Textiles* is a cowry shell, which in West Africa represents female genitalia and fertility and was also used as currency in the region before money was introduced by Europeans (p. 63). The cowry shell image speaks clearly to Ndiritu's themes of the commodification of African women's sexuality.[4] Her sensual movements evoke the erotic, but it is her textiles that locate her as an African woman.

Skirt panel, 20th century. Kuba people, Democratic Republic of the Congo. Raffia, plain weave with cut-pile embroidery. Private collection. These raffia dance skirts were woven in pieces by men using upright single-heddle looms, then sewn together and embroidered by women using a cut-pile technique. Women also used them in dances at rituals, and the skirts were stored and presented by family members at burials.

▶

Tiraz Fragment, 10th century. Abbasid period. Linen, paint, 9 x 14 in. The Metropolitan Museum of Art, New York, Gift of George D. Pratt, 1931 (31.106.32).

◀

Bushoong Kuba official in formal attire, Democratic Republic of the Congo, 1970s.

The Nigerian photographer Samuel Fosso also uses Dutch wax print fabrics in his more recent works. A commercial portrait photographer in Bangui, Fosso emerged from the West African studio photography tradition of using clothing and set decoration to convey messages about subjects' status and self-identity.[5] In the 1990s, Fosso was commissioned by a French department store to produce a series of advertising images. In *Le Chef*, Fosso recreates the iconic pose of an African chief seated in state upon a stool or chair, decked out in high-status cloth and expensive regalia of gold or cowry shells, feet resting on a cushion, holding a staff of authority in his hands and framed by a backdrop of special or significant fabric. By replacing the traditionally valuable objects within this scene with commercial European products, Fosso critiques the African chief who exploits his own people to gain wealth from the colonizers. Hence those Dutch-made or -inspired printed cloths are given pride of place as back-drop, the "chief" wears fake gold chains and sunglasses, and he holds a bunch of plastic sunflowers instead of a staff (p. 35). The only truly African-produced item in the scene is the Kuba embroidered pile cloth from the Congo under the chief's feet. Only by keeping Africa underfoot can the chief enjoy the fruits of a colonial relationship. Fosso's use of printed fabric with a mirror motif as a backdrop is telling: he is holding a mirror to the exploitative African chief.

Fosso's *La Femme libérée américaine dans les années 70* represents his vision of the emancipated African-American woman of the 1970s, unfettered by social constraints on her sexuality or economic power (p. 40).[6] To evoke this woman, he dresses in a pantsuit made of a patchwork of Dutch wax print cloth, with stiletto heels and a jaunty straw hat. However, the outfit is like nothing an African-American woman would actually wear. With his limited experience of American culture, Fosso's choices instead reflect his own West African culture. The suit he wears would never be worn by a woman, since women in West Africa do not wear trousers. Perhaps instead of a "liberated American woman," this image reveals a glimpse of how an African woman might look if granted the same freedoms as an American woman. To indicate her liberation, Fosso's woman wears men's clothing.

Women's Voices

Gender is another primary personal attribute conveyed by textiles and dress traditions. A Moroccan woman living in the United States, Lalla Essaydi creates richly textured photographic portraits of Moroccan women surrounded by inscribed cloth. She uses calligraphy, a man's art, in henna painting, a woman's art, to write her diary on the cloth she drapes around her models and on her sets.[7] Designs painted on women's bodies in henna paste are an ancient form of decoration practiced widely in Hindu and Islamic cultures. This practice is intimately associated with women's life stage rituals such as puberty rites, weddings and childbirth.[8] The traditional designs are associated with fertility and although meaningful and communicative, are not linguistic.

Linguistic inscriptions on textiles have a long history in the Islamic world, beginning with tiraz fabrics produced for early and medieval Islamic courts.[9] These tiraz were embroidered or woven with calligraphic inscriptions glori-

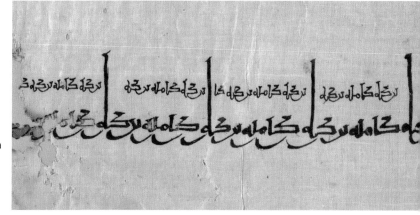

fying Allah and their patron caliph, who gave the cloth to his vassals and household to be worn as a sign of loyalty. Textiles, as one of the most portable and publicly visible media, were the ideal means to communicate political power across a ruler's lands and beyond. As weaving technology evolved, inscriptions on silk textiles became ever more elaborate. Some inscriptions became decorative elements in their own right and were often not legible. At the same time, inscriptions remained a primary design element on textiles used in religious contexts, since most Islamic traditions eschew representational imagery. Even today, the Ka'ba stone in Mecca is covered with a cloth inscribed with calligraphic blessings to Allah every year during the *hajj* (pilgrimage) period. Throughout their history,

inscribed Islamic textiles have been designed, produced and displayed by men. Essaydi appropriates this form of text on cloth from the public male space of political and religious power in the Islamic world to talk about her private experience as a woman in that world.

Henna painting is usually done during festive parties of mothers, daughters, aunts, sisters and other women in the private women's areas of the home, with the participants sharing stories, thoughts and dreams while painting the célèbre. Once painted, a woman's body is visible only to her husband within the home and is covered with clothing when she is outside the home. By transferring the henna painting from body to cloth and the painted marks from decorative symbols to communicative text, Essaydi takes her personal stories from the private, intimate women's space into the publicly visible male arena.

American Connections

Many of the artists in this exhibition deal with connections between North American and other cultures, as they observe them within the continent and elsewhere. iona rozeal brown, for example, takes as her inspiration a subculture among Japanese youth who don blackface and imitate African-American street culture.[10] Her works depict Japanese youth in the flat style of ukiyo-e woodblock prints, but she inserts markers of black urban identity into her images. Historically, Japanese clothing has reflected an elaborate code of colors, fabrics, motifs and garment forms that indicate the wearers' status, gender and age, as well as the seasons of the year and specific occasions.[11] In *a3 blackface #67*, brown translates this visual code into urban American street code, with an afro pick motif on the hairdresser's kimono, while his client sports a leopard-print hoodie with furry pink trim (p. 65).

Like brown, Mark Bradford explores intersections between African-American and Asian cultures. Bradford's *Miss China Silk* examines African-American women's use of supplemental hair, called weaves or extensions, which are made from Asian women's hair grown and sold specifically for this market (p. 64).[12] Bradford makes this connection explicit by depicting Asian-American women wearing Asian hair intended for African-Americans, while draped in cloth iconic of either the African- or Asian-American communities. While we might expect to see an Asian-American woman wearing the Chinese celebratory red silk fabric with its gold-brocade calligraphic roundels as in one of Bradford's images, the yellow cloth in two others

is a printed imitation of Ghanaian kente cloth. Kente was one of the first African textiles widely seen in the United States, when the president of newly independent Ghana visited the United Nations in New York in 1958, and it has since become a ubiquitous symbol of African-American identity.[13] In Ghana, kente is a woven cloth worn by Asante and Ewe kings and other high-ranking people. Bradford's commercially printed imitation kente connects his Asian women, with their headdress-like plumes of hair, to the African-American community.

In exploring his African-American identity, Willie Cole has looked to African objects such as carved wooden masks for inspiration, as well as to found objects around his home in Newark, New Jersey. Among the objects he finds, Cole has been especially attracted to irons throughout his life. His grandmother took in ironing; his studio is located in a former iron workshop; and abandoned irons serendipitously appear just when he most needs them for his work.[14] Is it a coincidence then that his iron-scorched flat pieces recall *bogolan*, the mudcloth from Mali, in their black and tan coloration and geometric layouts? Bogolan is produced by dyeing cloth in a yellow solution, then painting on an iron-rich mud that acts as a mordant to produce a strong, fast black dye and finally bleaching the unpainted areas white.[15] Among the Bamana in Mali, bogolan is a sacred cloth with powerful protective qualities, worn by hunters in the jungle and women in childbirth.[16] Since the 1990s, urban artists in Mali have produced artistic versions of mudcloth, and it has become one of the most iconic types of African textiles overseas. Commercially printed imitation and even mass-produced genuine mudcloth can be purchased on the street in many American cities. The colors and bold graphical quality of Cole's works reference Africa through these fabrics, while the scorched imprints of irons mirror their iron-mordanted dye.

Brian Jungen's Blankets comment in multiple ways on the interactions between Native Americans and Europeans, and on his experience identifying with both cultures (pp. 47 and 56). Jungen speaks of ceremonial dancing blankets as an invented tradition among his mother's Dane-zaa Nation tribe in British Columbia, created to appease the European-American desire for flamboyant exoticism.[17] Participants in Dane-zaa religious ceremonies to this day wear the traditional tunics and leggings of this circumpolar culture. In a separate, secular competitive dancing tradition developed for the benefit of outside observers, however, they wear large fringed mantles.

The Great Mosque at Mecca, crowded with pilgrims.

Kente Cloth (detail), 20th century. Ashanti people, Southern Ghana. Fabric, 152 x 112 in. The Newark Museum, Gift of Mr. and Mrs. William U. Wright, 1985 (85.366).

Guancha Diarra. Woman's Wrapped Skirt (detail), 1985. Bamana people, Mali. Painted cotton (*bokolanfini*) [also *bogolan*], 35 3/4 x 62 in. The Newark Museum (86.47).

Ceremonial Cape, 19th century. Chilkat people, Northwest Coast of North America. Cedar bark, wool, mountain goat hair; twined tapestry, 54 1/4 x 65 in. Musée du Quai Branly, Paris (71.1885.78.450).

Chief's Mantle, late 19th century. Halkomelem or Stalo people (Coast Salish culture), Musqueam, British Columbia. Mountain goat hair; twill weave with weft twined tapestry borders. Royal British Columbia Museum (1189).

Outsiders probably expected flashy dancing blankets from the Dane-zaa because of the centrality of such mantles to ceremonial practice among many neighboring groups to the east and south of the Dane-zaa homeland on the northwest coast of North America.

When Europeans arrived in the Pacific Northwest in the eighteenth century, they found a thriving local population and trade network. Spectacular mantles worn by high-ranking men during ceremonial dances were traded and given among clans during feasts, and they served as a form of wealth in themselves.[18] Tlingit Chilkat weavers produced the most prestigious mantles in twined tapestry, which allowed patterning, and these mantles were traded to many other groups in the area. Europeans plugged into this existing trade network, exchanging beads, buttons and commercial wool cloth and blankets for furs. The newly available materials were soon incorporated into local traditions: Haida women created mantles by sewing buttons onto the wool cloth, and Salish weavers used torn strips of red and blue wool cloth to create large plaid patterns in their twill-woven white mountain-goat hair blankets.[19]

Jungen's Blankets are most reminiscent of these Salish blankets because he uses both a twill weave construction and strips of existing cloth as a raw materials. By using strips cut from contemporary professional sports jerseys to construct his Native American-inspired mantles, Jungen highlights the "tribal" nature of contemporary sports teams and their fans, as well as the commercialization of Native practices.

Fashioning Identity

James Gobel's felt mosaics *The Fitting No.1* and *The Fitting No. 2* explore the role of homosexual male identity within fashion culture (p. 41).[20] Gobel's work centers on "bears," a gay subculture in the United States that rejects the young, buff, smooth, groomed, hip ideal of mainstream gay culture in favor of a more realistic, mundane version of masculinity. They celebrate maleness, not "gayness." As is typical in most gay subcultures, identity as a bear is signaled through an elaborate code of clothing and personal appearance.[21] Gobel's men display all the classic bear signs: a beard, plaid flannel shirt, Levi's jeans, work boots, chain wallet and leather wrist cuff. These garments reflect working-class American men's clothing worn for manly, physical occupations such as logging, mechanical work, hunting or farming. The antithesis of the ever-changing fashion world, this work uniform has changed very little over the past century or more.

By situating his bears in a fashion industry setting, Gobel displaces the stereotype of a flamingly effeminate gay fashion maven. These men work dispassionately, as if at their blue-collar jobs, rather than as over-the-top fashionistas. The visual juxtaposition of the bears' utilitarian, never-changing work clothes and the model's delicate draped dress satirizes both the image of the "queer eye" in fashion and the place of high style in the gay community.

In his Soundsuits, Nick Cave transformed found sequined and beaded fabrics into elaborate collages in garment form, some with towering pointed headdresses (p. 44). The found fabrics represent discarded special occasion garb and performance costumes fashioned to bestow glamour upon their wearers. Trained as a fashion designer, Cave speaks of the found fabrics as transmitting the energy of their former makers and wearers into his artwork.[22] The attire in his Soundsuits is meant to be worn in

The Thornton Portrait Gallery in the Huntington Art Gallery at the Huntington Library, Art Collections, and Botanical Gardens, Pasadena, California.

performance, subsuming the wearer's identity within the multiple voices of the fabrics. The peaked shape of the headdresses recalls other transformational performance headgear, from African masks that evoke spirits in cere-monial dances to identity-concealing KKK hoods in the United States and even miters worn by bishops and other clergy during high church ceremonies.

Defining Space

Textiles used to furnish interior spaces extend the same issues of social identity communicated by clothing beyond the body and into the environment. Furnishing fabrics render spaces habitable, both in terms of physical comfort and utility and as appropriate social settings for the unfolding of human interactions.

The glorious hodge-podge of color and pattern in Mickalene Thomas's works comes in large part from the furnishing fabrics in her sets. Her rhinestone-encrusted paintings are based on studio photographs of African-American women situated within backdrops designed to inspire the models to reveal their true selves.[23] The models in *Girlfriends and Lovers* strike self-assured poses in a set draped in boldly patterned 1960s and 1970s interior fabrics (p. 33). The striped fabric in the center background bears Egyptian-esque symbols, a nod to the Africanist sensibilities in the African-American community of the 1970s, while the other large-scale stylized patterns and the Persian-inspired tablecloth were associated with an avant-garde, youthful, or counterculture clientele, reflecting then-current fashion and a reaction against the floral chintzes of affluent mainstream interiors.[24] These fabrics were favored by many African-Americans as part of a distinct aesthetic that first emerged in the wake of the civil rights era. The bold patterns of this setting were hip around 1972. In 2008, the dated fabrics might suggest a struggle beneath the models' confidence, as if their setting was furnished from a thrift store or their parents' homes, unchanged for thirty-six years.

Kehinde Wiley references interior furnishing fabrics in a different way. The backgrounds of his portraits of contemporary young African-American men in iconic poses from Old Master paintings are filled with patterns drawn from furnishing textiles of the past several centuries. In those eras, the paintings he appropriates for his contem-porary portraits would have been displayed in the salons of wealthy homes, hung on walls covered with silk damask or brocade textiles. Wiley saw Old Master paintings hung in such an environment as a child when he visited the Huntington Art Gallery in San Marino, California.[25]

The wealthy subjects of the historic paintings that Wiley references lived in such spaces, but the backgrounds in their portraits typically pictured landscapes or formal drapery. By replacing those backgrounds with patterns based on silk wall coverings, Wiley situates his contemporary urban African-American subjects within

the manor house salon environment that their poses suggest. The floral ogival lattice in the background of Wiley's *The Blessing Christ* (p. 66) and neoclassical scrolling acanthus leaves of *Alexander the Great* (p. 34) are precisely the sorts of patterns that adorned those silk wall coverings, although Wiley admits that he will "sex up" the colors and scale of the patterns to suit his contemporary eye.[26] The sinuous floral tendrils of the textile designs escape from the background to caress and envelop the figures, drawing them deeper into the white European world of wealth and power.

Each of the artists in *Pattern ID* uses textiles or dress traditions in his or her art to indicate or challenge identity in some way. Grace Ndiritu's printed cloth and Kehinde Wiley's furnishing silks firmly situate their work within a specific cultural setting. James Gobel juxtaposes textiles from two disparate milieus to point up the differences between those worlds, while Brian Jungen's convergence of textile material from one culture and form from another reveals similarities between the two. By appropriating textile forms across geographic and gender boundaries, Yinka Shonibare and Lalla Essaydi manifest heretofore invisible identities.

Within a visual context, be it art or life itself, textiles are an immediate and powerful communicator of many aspects of personal identity, and they may be manipulated or selected to construct an identity at will. The primacy of textiles among trade goods since ancient times has fueled this process of reinventing identity throughout history. As textiles continue to migrate across geographic, cultural and social boundaries, they expand the possible identities their users may assume. We truly are what we wear.

Notes

1 See Mary Schoeser, *World Textiles: A Concise History* (London: Thames and Hudson, 2003).
2 See John Picton, "Laughing at Ourselves," in *Yinka Shonibare: Double Dutch*, ed. Jaap Guidemond, Gabriele Mackert, and Barbera van Kooij (Rotterdam: Museum Boijmans Van Beuningen; Vienna: Kunsthalle Wien; Rotterdam: Nai Publishers, 2004).
3 Rachel Kent, "Time and Transformation in the Art of Yinka Shonibare MBE," in *Yinka Shonibare MBE* (Munich, New York: Prestel, 2008), 12.
4 Melissa Gronlund, "Grace Ndiritu," *Frieze* 107 (May 2007).
5 Maria Francesca Bonetti, "Samuel Fosso: Studio Photographer in Baugui," in *Samuel Fosso*, ed. Maria Francesca Bonetti and Guido Schlinkert (Milan: 5 Continents, 2004), 58.
6 Guido Schlinkert, "Transformer," in ibid., 51.
7 Lalla Essaydi, in Amanda Carlson, *Lalla Essaydi: Converging Territories* (New York: powerHouse Books, 2005), 28.
8 Loretta Roome, *Mendhi: The Timeless Art of Henna Painting* (New York: St. Martin's Griffin, 1998), 30.
9 Sheila S. Blair, *Islamic Inscriptions* (New York: New York University Press, 1998), 165.
10 Benjamin Genocchio, "For Japanese Girls, Black Is Beautiful," *New York Times*, April 4, 2004.

11 Shigeki Kawakami, "Clad in Beautiful Colors and Myriad Motifs," in *Classical Kimono from the Kyoto National Museum* (San Francisco: Asian Art Museum of San Francisco, 1997), 23–26.
12 Mark Bradford, artist's statement, 2009, unpublished.
13 Doran Ross, *Wrapped in Pride: Ghanaian Kente and African-American Identity* (Los Angeles: UCLA Fowler Museum of Cultural History, 1998), 166.
14 Patterson Sims, ed., *Anxious Objects: Willie Cole's Favorite Brands* (New Brunswick, N.J.: Rutgers University Press, 2006), 22.
15 John Picton and John Mack, *African Textiles* (London: British Museum Publications Ltd., 1979), 161.
16 Victoria Rovine, "Fashionable Traditions: The Globalization of an African Textile," in Jean Allman, ed., *Fashioning Africa: Power and the Politics of Dress* (Bloomington and Indianapolis: Indiana University Press, 2004), 194.
17 Jessica Morgan, "Out of Bounds: Brian Jungen," Qvest.com, 2008, http://91.186.11.41/qvest/home/art/ggbrian-jungen (accessed June 10, 2009).
18 Cheryl Samuel, *The Chilkat Dancing Blanket* (Seattle: Pacific Search Press, 1982), 35.
19 Paula Gustafson, *Salish Weaving* (Vancouver: Douglas & McIntyre; Seattle:

University of Washington Press, 1980), 59.
20 Nayland Blake, *James Gobel* (Los Angeles: UCLA Hammer Museum, 2000).
21 Ray Kampf, *The Bear Handbook: A Comprehensive Guide for Those Who Are Husky, Hairy, and Homosexual, and Those Who Love 'Em* (Haworth Press, 2000), 54–57.
22 James Sanders, *Nick Cave: Soundsuits* (Chicago: Department of Cultural Affairs, 2006).
23 Jeff Jahn, "What's next for Mickalene Thomas," http://www.portlandart.net/archives/2009/05/mickalene_thoma.html (accessed June 10, 2009).
24 Mary Schoeser and Celia Rufey, *English and American Textiles from 1790 to the Present* (New York: Thames and Hudson, 1989), 210–16.
25 Joe Houston, *Kehinde Wiley: Columbus* (Columbus, Ohio: Columbus Museum of Art; Los Angeles, California: Roberts & Tilton, 2006), 8.
26 Emil Wibekin, "Master Class," in ibid., 28.

Mark Bradford

Bradford, Mark. *Street Level: Mark Bradford, William Cordova, and Robin Rhode*. Ed. Trevor Schoonmaker. Durham: Nasher Museum of Art, 2007.

Foster, Carter E. *Neither New nor Correct: New Work by Mark Bradford*. New York: Whitney Museum of American Art; New Haven: Yale University Press, 2007.

iona rozeal brown

Genocchio, Benjamin. "For Japanese Girls, Black Is Beautiful" *New York Times*, April 4, 2004, section 2, 36.

Harris, Juliette. "Evolving in All Possible Directions" (editorial). *International Review of African American Art* 22/2 (2008): inside front cover, 22–23.

Nick Cave

Brown, Glen. "Irreducible Energy: Nick Cave." *Ornament* 31/2 (2007): 38–43.

Cave, Nick. *Meet Me at the Center of the Earth*. San Francisco: Yerba Buena Center for the Arts, 2009.

Nick Cave and Clarina Bezzola: Concealing & Revealing. Sheboygan: John Michael Kohler Arts Center, 2004.

Yood, James. "Nick Cave: Chicago Cultural Arts Center." *American Craft* 66/6 (December 2006/January 2007): 56–57.

Willie Cole

Cole, Willie. *Willie Cole*. St. Louis: St. Louis Art Museum, 1992.

Performance Anxiety: Angela Bulloch, Cai Guo Qiang, Willie Cole, Renee Green, Charles Long, Paul McCarthy, Julia Scher, Jim Shaw, Rirkrit Tiravanija. Chicago: Museum of Contemporary Art; New York: Distributed Art Publishers, 1997.

Sims, Patterson, ed. *Anxious Objects: Willie Cole's Favorite Brands*. New Brunswick: Rutgers University Press, 2006.

Lalla Essaydi

Carlson, Amanda. *Lalla Essaydi: Converging Territories*. New York: powerHouse Books, 2005.

Mernissi, Fatema. *Les Femmes du Maroc*. Brooklyn, N.Y.: powerHouse Books, 2009.

Miller, Francine Koslow. "Lalla Essaydi: Howard Yezerski Gallery." *Artforum International* 45/5 (January 2009): 216.

Whitley, Lauren. "Lalla Essaydi: Eloquent Cloth." *Fiberarts* 32/4 (January/February 2006): 42–43.

Samuel Fosso

Bonetti, Maria Francesca, and Guido Schinkert, ed. *Samuel Fosso*. Milan: 5 Continents, 2004.

Camhi, Leslie. "A Man of A Thousand Faces." *New York Times Magazine*. March 8, 2009, 82-84.

James Gobel

James Gobel. Los Angeles: Hammer Museum UCLA, 2000.

Miller, Leigh Anne. "James Gobel at Kravets Wehby." *Art in America* 93/11 (December 2005): 151.

Morris, Barbara. "James Gobel at Marx & Zavattero Gallery." *Artweek* 39/4 (May 2008): 13–14.

Brian Jungen

Brian Jungen. Vancouver, B.C.: Douglas & McIntyre; Berkeley, Calif.: Publishers Group West, 2005.

Jungen, Brian. *Brian Jungen*. Ed. Solange de Boer, Zoë Gray, and Nicolaus Schafhausen. Rotterdam: Witte de With Center for Contemporary Art, 2006.

Nadelman, Cynthia. "Tribal Hybrids." *ARTNews* 106/6 (June 2007): 122–27.

Sholis, Brian. "Brian Jungen: Casey Kaplan Gallery." *Artforum International* 46/10 (Summer 2008): 438–39.

Bharti Kher

Kher, Bharti. *Bharti Kher*. New York: Jack Shainman Gallery, 2007.

Mehta, Anupa. *India 20: Conversations with Contemporary Artists*. India: Mapin Publishing; Ocean Townshop, N.J.: Grantha; Easthampton, Mass.: Antique Collectors Club, 2007.

New Delhi New Wave. Ed. Jérôme Neutres. Bologna: Damiani Editore, 2007.

Ng, Elaine. "Bharti Kher." *Art AsiaPacific*, no. 61 (November/December 2008): 296–97.

Takashi Murakami

© *Murakami*. Ed. Paul Schimmel and Lisa Gabrielle Mark. Los Angeles: Museum of Contemporary Art; New York: Rizzoli International; Tokyo: Kaikai Kiki Co., 2007.

Cruz, Amada. *Takashi Murakami: The Meaning of the Nonsense of the Meaning*. New York: Center for Curatorial Studies, Bard College, 1999.

Murakami, Takashi. *Super Flat*. Tokyo: Madorashuppan, 2000.

Grace Ndiritu

Grace Ndiritu. Ed. Nigel Prince. Birmingham, Eng.: Ikon Gallery; Venice, Italy: Nuova Icona; Manchester, Eng.: Cornerhouse, 2005.

Gumpert, Lynn, ed. *The Poetics of Cloth: African Textiles/Recent Art*. New York: Grey Art Gallery, New York University, 2008.

Williams, Eliza. "Grace Ndiritu." *Flash Art International* 40 (July/September 2007): 135.

Yinka Shonibare, MBE

Shonibare, Yinka. *Yinka Shonibare: Double Dress*. Jerusalem: Israel Museum, 2002.

———. *Yinka Shonibare: Double Dutch*. Ed. Jaap Guidemond, Gabriele Mackert, and Barbera van Kooij. Rotterdam: Museum Boijmans Van Beuningen; Vienna: Kunsthalle Wien; Rotterdam: NAi Publishers, 2004.

———. *Yinka Shonibare: Garden of Love*. Paris: Musée du Quai Branly, 2007.

———. *Yinka Shonibare, MBE*. Munich; New York: Prestel, 2008.

Yinka Shonibare: Dressing Down. Birmingham, Eng.: Ikon Gallery, 1999.

Mickalene Thomas

Dailey, Meghan. "Mickalene Thomas." *Art & Auction* 32/7 (March 2009): 39–44.

Kino, Carol. "A Confidence Highlighted in Rhinestones." *New York Times,* April 12, 2009, AR 23.

Walker, Kara. "Mickalene Thomas." *Bomb,* no. 07 (Spring 2009): 73–74.

Aya Uekawa

Platow, Raphaela. *Aya Uekawa*. Cincinnati: Contemporary Arts Center, 2009.

Shiner, Eric C. "A Utopia Revisited: Aya Uekawa," *Juxtapoz* no. 96 (January 2009): 64-77

Shiner, Eric C., and Reiko Tomii. *Making a Home: Japanese Contemporary Artists in New York Exhibition Catalogue.* New York: Japan Society, 2007.

Kehinde Wiley

Fortune, Brandon Brame. *Recognize!: Hip Hop and Contemporary Portraiture.* Washington, D.C.: National Portrait Gallery, Smithsonian Institution, 2008.

Houston, Joe. *Kehinde Wiley: Columbus.* Columbus, Ohio: Columbus Museum of Art; Los Angeles: Roberts & Tilton, 2006.

Neo Baroque! Ed. Micaela Giovannotti and Joyce B. Korotkin. Milan: Charta, 2005.

Wiley, Kehinde. *Black Light.* Brooklyn, N.Y.: powerHouse Books, 2009.

———. *Kehinde Wiley: The World Stage: China.* Sheboygan: John Michael Kohler Arts Center, 2007.

———. *Passing Posing Paintings & Faux Chapel.* New York: Distributed Art Publishers, 2005.

———. *The World Stage: Africa, Lagos/Dakar.* New York: Studio Museum Harlem, 2008.

Additional Resources

Allman, Jean, ed. *Fashioning Africa: Power and the Politics of Dress.* Bloomington and Indianapolis: Indiana University Press, 2004.

Blair, Sheila S. *Islamic Inscriptions.* New York: New York University Press, 1998.

Colchester, Chloe. *Textiles Today: A Global Survey of Trends and Traditions.* New York: Thames and Hudson, 2007.

Gentz, Natascha, and Stefan Kramer, ed. *Globalization, Cultural Identities, and Media Representations.* Albany: SUNY, 2006.

Gustafson, Paula. *Salish Weaving.* Vancouver: Douglas & McIntyre; Seattle: University of Washington Press, 1980.

Hetherington, Kevin. *Expressions of Identity: Space, Performance, Politics.* London: Sage Publications, 1998.

Kampf, Ray. *The Bear Handbook: A Comprehensive Guide for Those Who Are Husky, Hairy, and Homosexual, and Those Who Love 'Em.* Philadelphia: Haworth Press, 2000.

Livingstone, Joan, and John Ploof, ed. *The Object of Labor: Art, Cloth, and Cultural Production.* Chicago: School of the Art Institute of Chicago Press; Cambridge, Mass.: MIT Press, 2007.

Morrison, Michael, and Lorna Price, ed. *Classical Kimono from the Kyoto National Museum.* San Francisco: Asian Art Museum of San Francisco, 1997.

Paulicelli, Eugenia, and Hazel Clark, ed. *The Fabric of Cultures: Fashion, Identity, and Globalization.* New York: Routledge, 2009.

Picton, John, and John Mack. *African Textiles.* London: British Museum Publications Ltd., 1979.

Roach-Higgins, Mary Ellen, Joanne B. Eicher, and Kim K. P. Johnson, ed. *Dress and Identity.* New York: Fairchild Publications, 2009.

Roome, Loretta. *Mendhi: The Timeless Art of Henna Painting.* New York: St. Martin's Griffin, 1998.

Ross, Doran. *Wrapped in Pride: Ghanaian Kente and African-American Identity.* Los Angeles: UCLA Fowler Museum of Cultural History, 1998.

Samuel, Cheryl. *The Chilkat Dancing Blanket.* Seattle: Pacific Search Press, 1982.

Schoeser, Mary. *World Textiles: A Concise History.* London: Thames and Hudson, 2003.

Schoeser, Mary, and Celia Rufey. *English and American Textiles from 1790 to the Present.* New York: Thames and Hudson, 1989.

Van der Plas, Els, and Marlous Willemsen, ed., *The Art of African Fashion.* The Hague, The Netherlands: Prince Claus Fund, 1998.

Walker, Sheila, ed., *African Root/American Cultures: Africa in the Creation of the Americas.* Lanham, Md.: Rowman & Littlefield, 2001.

Wood, Joe. "The Yellow Negro." *Transition,* no. 73 (1997), 40–66.

The Cultural Currency of Pattern and Dress

Holbein, Hans the Younger: *The Ambassadors*: National Gallery, London/ Art Resource, N.Y.; *The Dead Christ*: Erich Lessing/Art Resource, N.Y.

Matisse, Henri: *Reclining Odalisque in Gray Culottes*: © The Metropolitan Museum of Art/Art Resource, N.Y.; *Still Life in Seville I*: Cameraphoto Arte, Venice/Art Resource, N.Y.; *The Pink Studio (Studio of the Painter)*: SCALA/Art Resource, N.Y.

Schapiro, Miriam: *Wonderland*: Smithsonian American Art Museum, Washington, D.C./Art Resource, N.Y.

Boit, Charles, *Augustus II the Strong*: Jürgen Karpinski/Bildarchiv Preussischer Kulturbesitz /Art Resource, N.Y.

Utamaro, Kitagawa: *from the series "Twelve Female Professions:" The Hairdresser*, Reunion des Museés Nationaux/Art Resource, N.Y.

Rembrandt, Harmensz van Rijn: *The Syndics of the Amsterdam Drapers' Guild*: Bildarchiv Preussischer Kulturbesitz/Art Resource, N.Y.

Picasso, Pablo: *Les Demoiselles D'Avignon*: The Museum of Modern Art/ Licensed by SCALA/Art Resource, N.Y.

Ingres, Jean Auguste Dominique: *The Great Odalisque*: Reunion des Museés Nationaux/Art Resource, N.Y.

Raphael: *The Three Graces*: Erich Lessing/ Art Resource, N.Y.

We Are What We Wear

Skirt panel, Kuba; Democratic Republic of the Congo: Werner Forman/Art Resource, N.Y.

Chilkat ceremonial cape: Musée du Quai Branly/Scala/Art Resource, N.Y., photo by Patrick Gvies/Bruno Descoings.

Tiraz fragment: © The Metropolitan Museum of Art/Art Resource, N.Y.

Raffia dance skirts: Werner Forman/Art Resource, N.Y.

Great Mosque at Mecca: © DeA Picture Library/Art Resource, N.Y.

Coast Salish chief's mantle: Image 5257-F courtesy Royal BC Museum, BC Archives.

Kente cloth, Ashanti People, Ghana: The Newark Museum/Art Resource, N.Y.

Woman's skirt (bogolanfini), detail: The Newark Museum/Art Resource, N.Y.

Dutch wax print cloth worn by women in market: © Francis Kennett. *Ethnic Dress*. New York: Facts on File, 1995.

Bushoong Kuba official in formal attire, Democratic Republic of the Congo, 1970s: © Monni Adams, Peabody Museum.

Thornton Portrait Gallery in the Huntington Art Gallery at The Huntington Library, Art Collections, and Botanical Gardens: Photo by John Edward Linden, © The Huntington Library, Art Collections, and Botanical Gardens.

Works in the exhibition

Bradford, Mark: *Miss China Silk,* 2005: courtesy Sikkema Jenkins & Co., New York.

brown, iona rozeal: *a3 blackface # 67*, 2003: courtesy the artist, photo by Brandon Webster; *a3 blackface #55,* 2003: courtesy the artist, photo by Andrew McAllister; *Introducing: Kaatchi the surrogate*; *Introducing: Kenna the siren, polyphony in G with moorfish*, 2008: courtesy the artist and Goff + Rosenthal.

Cave, Nick: *Soundsuits*, 2009; *Tondo,* 2009: courtesy the artist and James Prinz.

Cole, Willie: *Procession*, 2006: courtesy Alexander and Bonin, New York; *Garden (Ozone Summer Series)*, 1991: courtesy the Progressive Corporation.

Essaydi, Lalla: *Les Femmes du Maroc #26A*, 2006; *Les Femmes du Maroc: Grande Odalisque*, 2008; *Les Femmes du Maroc: Moorish Woman*, 2008;

Converging Territories #31, 2003: © Lalla Essaydi/courtesy Edwynn Houk Gallery, New York.

Fosso, Samuel: *Self Portrait*, 1977; *La Femme libérée américaine dans les années 70* [Liberated American Woman in the 70's], 1997: © Jack Shainman Gallery, New York, photo by Joe Levack; *Le Chef* [The Chief], 1997: © Samuel Fosso 2009, courtesy Jean Marc Patras/Paris

Gobel, James: *The Fitting No. 1*, 2007; *The Fitting No. 2*, 2007; *I'll Be Your Friend, I'll Be Your Love, I'll Be Everything You Need*, 2009: courtesy Kravets/Wehby, New York.

Jungen, Brian: *Blanket no. 6*, 2008; *Blanket no. 4*, 2008: courtesy the artist and Casey Kaplan, New York.

Kher, Bharti: *Mother of anything possible, anytime*, 2006; *Diamonds*, 2007: courtesy the artist and Jack Shainman Gallery, New York.

Murakami, Takashi: *Eye Love SUPERFLAT*, 2003: © 2003 Takashi Murakami/Kaikai Kiki Co., Ltd. All Rights Reserved; *Eye Love SUPERFLAT*, 2004: © 2004 Takashi Murakami/Kaikai Kiki Co., Ltd. All Rights Reserved; *Jellyfish Eyes*, 2002: © 2002 Takashi Murakami/Kaikai Kiki Co., Ltd. All Rights Reserved, photo by Andrew McAllister

Ndiritu, Grace: *Still Life*, 2005–7: courtesy Grace Ndiritu.

Shonibare, Yinka: *Three Graces*, 2001: courtesy the Speed Art Museum, Louisville, KY; *La Méduse*, 2008: © The artist, courtesy James Cohan Gallery, New York.

Thomas, Mickalene: *Girlfriends and Lovers,* 2008: courtesy the artist and Rhona Hoffman Gallery; *A Moments Pleasure #2*, 2008; *This Is Where I Came In*, 2006: courtesy the artist; *It Hurts So Good! (Brawlin' Spitfire Two)*, 2007: courtesy the artist and Susanne Vielmetter Projects.

Uekawa, Aya: *A Team Player Candidate (The Chicken Feather)*, 2004; *A Team Player Candidate (Pearl Necklaces)*, 2005;

A Team Player Candidate (The Charm Lover), 2005: courtesy Kravets/Wehby, New York.

Wiley, Kehinde: *The Blessing Christ*, 2007; *Alexander the Great*, 2007: courtesy the artist and Deitch Projects, New York; *The Dead Christ in the Tomb*, 2007; *Santos Dumont-The Father of Aviation III*, 2009: courtesy Roberts and Tilton, Culver City, California.

Artist headshots

Samuel **Fosso**: © Studio Convenance, Bangui CAR.

Kehinde **Wiley**: kwaku@kwakualston. com.

Nick **Cave**: courtesy the artist.

79

**Published on the occasion
of the exhibition**
Pattern ID,
January 23–May 9, 2010.

Published by the
Akron Art Museum
One South High
Akron, Ohio 44308
330.376.9185
www.AkronArtMuseum.org

Editing: Barbara J. Bradley,
Cleveland, Ohio
Design: Christopher Hoot,
Cuyahoga Falls, Ohio
Printing: Printing Concepts,
Hudson, Ohio, USA

ISBN: 978-0-940665-07-1

Library of Congress Control
Number: 2009911510